WITHDRAWN

The Columbus Academy
Reinberger Middle School Library
4300 Cherry Bottom Road
Gahanna, Ohio 43230

S0-BNV-573

The
Korean
Americans

By Jennifer C. Martin

LUCENT BOOKS
An imprint of Thomson Gale, a part of The Thomson Corporation

THOMSON

GALE™

Detroit • New York • San Francisco • San Diego • New Haven, Conn. • Waterville, Maine • London • Munich

© 2005 Thomson Gale, a part of The Thomson Corporation.

Thomson and Star Logo are trademarks and Gale and Lucent Books are registered trademarks used herein under license.

For more information, contact
Lucent Books
27500 Drake Rd.
Farmington Hills, MI 48331-3535
Or you can visit our Internet site at http://www.gale.com

ALL RIGHTS RESERVED.
No part of this work covered by the copyright hereon may be reproduced or used in any form or by any means—graphic, electronic, or mechanical, including photocopying, recording, taping, Web distribution, or information storage retrieval systems—without the written permission of the publisher.

Every effort has been made to trace the owners of copyrighted material.

LIBRARY OF CONGRESS CATALOGING-IN-PUBLICATION DATA

Martin, Jennifer C., 1973–
   The Korean Americans / by Jennifer C. Martin.
      p. cm. — (Immigrants in America)
Includes bibliographical references and index.
Contents: Battle for the hermit kingdom—A new beginning—The mainland and discrimination—Building communities—The second wave—Becoming Korean American—Korean American contributions—One hundred years of Korean Americans.
   Audience: Grades 7–8.
   ISBN 1-59018-079-8 (hardcover : alk. paper)
1. Korean Americans—History—Juvenile literature. 2. Korean Americans—Social conditions—Juvenile literature. 3. Immigrants—United States—History—Juvenile literature. 4. Korea—Emigration and immigration—History—Juvenile literature. 5. United States—Emigration and immigration—History—Juvenile literature. I. Title. II. Series.
   E184.K6M27 2006
   973'.04957—dc22
                                                                              2004019816

Printed in the United States of America

CONTENTS

Foreword 4

Introduction
Fulfilling a Dream 6

Chapter One
Battle for the Hermit Kingdom 8

Chapter Two
A New Beginning 21

Chapter Three
The Mainland and Discrimination 33

Chapter Four
Building Communities 44

Chapter Five
The Second Wave 57

Chapter Six
Becoming Korean American 70

Chapter Seven
Korean American Contributions 84

Epilogue
One Hundred Years of Korean Americans 97

Notes 100
For Further Reading 103
Works Consulted 104
Index 108
Picture Credits 112
About the Author 112

Immigrants have come to America at different times, for different reasons, and from many different places. They leave their homelands to escape religious and political persecution, poverty, war, famine, and countless other hardships. The journey is rarely easy. Sometimes, it entails a long and hazardous ocean voyage. Other times, it follows a circuitous route through refugee camps and foreign countries. At the turn of the twentieth century, for instance, Italian peasants, fleeing poverty, boarded steamships bound for New York, Boston, and other eastern seaports. And during the 1970s and 1980s, Vietnamese men, women, and children, victims of a devastating war, began arriving at refugee camps in Arkansas, Pennsylvania, Florida, and California, en route to establishing new lives in the United States.

Whatever the circumstances surrounding their departure, the immigrants' journey is always made more difficult by the knowledge that they leave behind family, friends, and a familiar way of life. Despite this, immigrants continue to come to America because, for many, the United States represents something they could not find at home: freedom and opportunity for themselves and their children.

No matter what their reasons for emigrating, where they have come from, or when they left, once here, nearly all immigrants face considerable challenges in adapting and making the United States their new home. Language barriers, unfamiliar surroundings, and sometimes hostile neighbors make it difficult for immigrants to assimilate into American society. Some Vietnamese, for instance, could not read or write in their native tongue when they arrived in the United States. This heightened their struggle to communicate with employers who demanded they be literate in English, a language vastly different from their own. Likewise, Irish immigrant school children in Boston faced classmates who teased and belittled their lilting accent. Immigrants from Russia often felt isolated, having settled in areas of the United States where they had no access to traditional Russian foods. Similarly, Italian families, used to certain wines and spices, rarely shopped or traveled outside of New York's Little Italy, a self-contained community cut off from the rest of the city.

Even when first-generation immigrants do successfully settle into life in the United States, their children, born in America, often have different values and are influenced more by their country of birth than their parents' traditions. Children want to be a part of the American culture and usually welcome American ideals, beliefs, and styles. As they become more Americanized—adopting Western dating habits and fashions, for instance—they tend to cast aside or even actively reject the traditions embraced by their parents. Assimilation, then, often becomes an ideological dispute that creates conflict among immigrants of every ethnicity. Whether Chinese, Italian, Russian, or Vietnamese, young people battle their elders for respect, individuality, and freedom, issues that often would not have come up in their homeland. And no matter how tightly the first generations hold onto their traditions, in the end, it is usually the young people who decide what to keep and what to discard.

The Immigrants in America series fully examines the immigrant experience. Each book in the series discusses why the immigrants left their homeland, what the journey to America was like, what they experienced when they arrived, and the challenges of assimilation. Each volume includes discussion of triumph and tragedy, contributions and influences, history and the future. Fully documented primary and secondary source quotations enliven the text. Sidebars highlight interesting events and personalities. Annotated bibliographies offer ideas for additional research. Each book in this dynamic series provides students with a wealth of information as well as launching points for further discussion.

INTRODUCTION

Fulfilling a Dream

The dawn of the twentieth century brought the first Korean immigrants to America. Years of war and foreign dominance in Korea left the people persecuted and impoverished. In search of a better life, some Koreans journeyed to Hawaii and the United States seeking wealth and freedom.

After their arrival, Korean immigrants discovered the golden image of America was a dream. Faced with difficult labor and low wages, they struggled to survive while facing competition and hostility from white Americans and other Asians. Despite overwhelming odds, Korean Americans were able to build a home in America.

Against the Odds

The story of Korean Americans is one of hope and determination. Entering the United States near the height of Asian discrimination in the late nineteenth and early twentieth centuries, they soon found themselves unable to secure homes, farms, and businesses. Their reluctant status as citizens of Japan left them facing distrust and hostility. Despite being considered enemies by other Americans, their pride in America and their homeland drove them to support the war effort through volunteer work, financial aid, and military contributions.

The Korean American community banded together, forming a tightly woven alliance of religious, social, and business organizations. Working together, Korean Americans supported each other, pooling their resources to build businesses, schools, and communities. This unique cohesiveness allowed the Korean Americans to thrive even though they faced rigid restrictions from American society.

With the outbreak of the Korean War in 1950, thousands of Koreans fled to the United States. From war brides and refugees to orphans and scholars, these new immigrants changed the face of the Korean American community. The second wave injected new life into the Korean population as women and children entered the community. An increase in skilled professionals also increased the level of medical and legal services to the Korean community.

Today, urban areas like New York and Los Angeles boast booming Koreatowns—enclaves or neighborhoods with a large concentration of Korean American residents. Significant populations are also found in Honolulu, Chicago, Houston, and Seattle. Over 1 million Koreans call America home, with another 152,000 claiming mixed ancestry. As their population continues to grow, Korean Americans are finding visibility outside their communities in America's mainstream society.

Success has not come without a price. The rise of Korean American businesses has left the community struggling with the identity of a model minority. Korean immigrants and their children struggle with what it means to be Korean in America as they try to find the balance between tradition and assimilation.

With the rapid growth of the numbers of Korean American students attending universities, they are poised to become the new face of American leadership. Through their hard work and determination, Korean Americans are slowly realizing their American dream.

A young Korean American woman dressed in traditional clothing celebrates her heritage during the annual Korean Day parade in New York City.

CHAPTER ONE

Battle for the Hermit Kingdom

N amed Choson, the "Land of Morning Calm," by its people, the Korean Peninsula has a history that is far from serene. Korea has been embroiled in political struggle for most of its five-thousand-year history. With fertile rice fields and abundant natural resources such as coal, lead, copper, tungsten, and gold, Koreans have fought against invaders, including the Mongols, Chinese, Russians, Japanese, and Manchu, for centuries. Over nine hundred invasions were recorded in two thousand years of written history as neighboring countries sought control over this Minnesota-sized country. Invasions eventually led the Korean government in the early seventeenth century to deny access to all foreigners except those from China, earning Korea the nickname of the "Hermit Kingdom."

With more than 5,000 miles of coastline, Korea is a strategic military and commercial outpost. Bordering Russia and China, the peninsula is also a pathway to reaching the Japanese islands. The distance between Japan's Tsushima Islands, and Korea's closest island is just 21 miles. The Korean port of Pusan lies only 124 miles across the Strait of Korea from Fukuoka, Japan.

In the middle of the nineteenth century, Asian and Western powers competed for mastery over Korea. As these struggles intensified, Koreans began to look to other lands to find security and peace. At the dawn of the twentieth century, thousands of Koreans journeyed to the United States to escape political oppression.

Confucian Tradition

For centuries, a mixture of Buddhism, Confucianism, and Taoism influenced Korean society. First introduced in the tenth century, Confucianism was adopted as the state religion at the close of the fourteenth century. Followers of Confucianism believe the superior person esteems education and enlightenment, while the lesser person seeks wealth and profit. Universal harmony is achieved by recognizing de-

fined societal roles and maintaining individual conformity to those roles.

A strict social structure was developed to describe these roles, including subordinate relationships within the family and society as a whole. For example, children were expected to defer to their fathers, women to men, and lower classes to upper. The Korean king was at the highest point in the social structure and was believed to be the center of the universe, subordinate only to the Chinese emperor. Below the king was the *yangban*, or scholar class. The *yangban* held government offices and were expected to look after the masses as a father would a child.

The *chungin* were the middle class. These were usually members of a lower family and

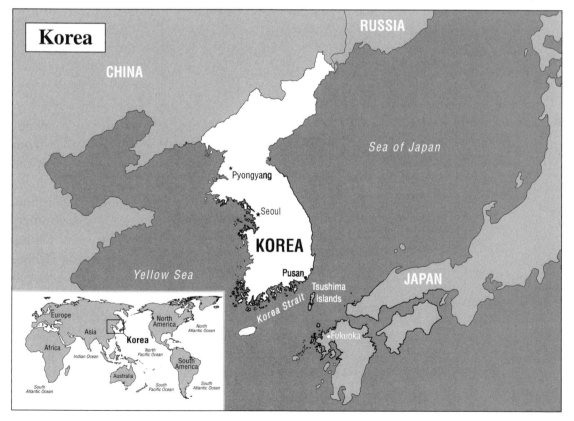

held positions such as artists, physicians, and administrators. The *chungin* served as regional governors and were the link between the masses and the upper class. Commoners, such as farmers and merchants, were called the *sangmin*. The *sangmin* were the largest class, about 75 percent of the population, and bore the brunt of taxation. The lowest class was the *ch'ommin*, literally meaning the "despised people." These were slaves, servants, actors, jailors, butchers, and others engaged in what were considered "unclean" occupations. When Koreans met one another, they were expected to speak and act according to their rank.

The social hierarchy was illustrated through dress and color. Most Korean adults wore white. Members of the nobility and other high-ranking officials wore rich colors like red, blue, and purple to denote their status. The peasantry's garments were made of hemp or cotton, while fabrics such as silk were reserved for the privileged class. Accessories also proclaimed social status. Members of the *yangban* wore special hats, the different shapes indicating family or employment status, and elegant shoes. Average citizens wore plain caps made of horsehair and shoes made of straw or rubber.

This Confucian ideal even extended beyond the Korean social structure to relationships between countries. When making decisions the Korean government deferred to more powerful or influential countries. For example, Korea was considered a subordinate state to China, the birthplace of Confucianism. This practice of subservience, called *sadaejuui* or *sadae sasang*, relied on a stronger power to ensure Korean independence. This hierarchical system would influence Korea's political relationships for centuries.

In nineteenth-century Confucian society, the yangban, *or scholar class, wore hats of different shapes to symbolize their social status.*

Isolationism

Following invasions by the Japanese in 1592, and by the Manchus (from the northeastern part of China known as Manchuria) in 1627 and 1636, Korea developed a mistrust of outsiders and sealed itself off from foreign influence for 250 years. Its closest ties were to its neighbor China. Sharing common technology and religion, Korea had long been considered China's "Little Brother." In the Confucian tradition, the Chinese emperor was the center of the universe, and all other persons were subordinate to his power. The Korean monarchy sent annual tributes to the Chinese emperor to ensure a peaceful relationship between the two countries. Although the Korean government managed its own affairs, the Chinese frequently aided in the political arena.

In 1864, an eleven-year-old boy named Kojong ascended the Korean throne. His father was Yi Ha-ung (Prince Hungson), brother of the late king. Due to King Kojong's tender age, Yi Ha-ung was granted the title *taewon-gun* (grand prince). *Taewon-gun* acted as prince regent, ruling in his son's stead. During this time China and Japan began to open themselves up to Western trade. However, the grand prince did not follow their lead and supported continued isolationism. His policy has been summarized by author Bruce Cumings as "no treaties, no trade, no Catholics, no West, and no Japan."[1]

As Kojong grew older, power struggles frequently erupted between the isolationist *taewon-gun* and the pro-West King Kojong and his wife, Queen Min. Several times during Kojong's rule the *taewon-gun*, the king, or the queen fled the palace as rivaling factions forced their way into power. These internal struggles weakened the Korean government and left the country open to foreign exploitation.

Western Encroachment

Despite Korea's isolationism, Western ideas and technology entered the kingdom through China. One of the most influential doctrines was that of Christianity. Since the 1780s, Christian missionaries from France and the United States petitioned the Korean government for entrance into Korea. The requests were repeatedly denied. To the *yangban* elite, the Catholic loyalty to the pope conflicted with loyalty to the Korean king and nobility. A deviation from the Confucian ideal would lead to a breakdown in longstanding cultural norms and undermine the *yangban*'s authority.

Since the *yangban* believed themselves superior to the lower classes, if Christianity was accepted, some feared lower classes would see themselves as equals to the aristocrats and perhaps even aspire to professions reserved for the upper classes. The pampered wealthy class did not want their life of privilege threatened by Christian influences.

Despite government efforts, Christianity did come to Korea. For the Korean peasantry, the Christian promise of equality among all men and women was an improvement over Confucianism's hierarchy. Thousands of Korean peasants abandoned Confucianism for Christianity. The Korean monarchy struggled to contain the growing

King Kojong and his wife Queen Min wished to open Korea up to Western trade, just as China and Japan had done earlier in the nineteenth century.

numbers of Christians by banning Christian missionaries. Catholic priests ignored the ban and sneaked across the borders, aided by Korean converts.

As the number of Christians continued to grow, the government's policy of suppression quickly turned to extermination. By 1801, the government began massacring converts, hoping to contain the threat and maintain control over the people. The murders increased throughout the first half of the 1800s. In the 1860s alone, over eight thousand converts were report-

edly slaughtered. After three French priests were killed, France sent troops to halt the murders. The Korean monarch responded by sending twenty thousand soldiers to defeat the French invaders.

The Opening of Korea

Despite the Korean government's harsh reaction to the French presence and continued refusal to entertain Western trade talks, the United States exhibited interest in trading with the Hermit Kingdom and sent naval ships to Korea. With Korea's volatile history, the appearance of foreign warships raised fears of invasion among many Koreans. Christianity was causing enough problems for the government in Korea; the Korean government was determined to prevent further foreign influence and declined trade negotiations. Despite the Korean resolve against trade, the U.S. government was determined to force trade.

In 1866, a heavily armed U.S. trade ship, the *General Sherman*, sailed toward the Korean capital at Pyongyang to force negotiations. After the *Sherman*'s crew kidnapped a local official, a Korean mob arrived to protest the ship's presence and demand the official's release. Fearing an attack, the Americans opened fire and wounded several Koreans. When low tide arrived, the Koreans attacked the stranded *Sherman*, burning the ship and killing the crew. Five years later, in 1871, 650 American sailors and marines landed at Kanghwa, an island in the Yellow Sea off Korea's western coast, to avenge the *Sherman's* crew. As many as 600 Korean soldiers lost their lives driving off the invaders.

In all, seven French and five American ships were driven from the Korean coast

---

Ransoming Relics

The Korean government's refusal to trade with other countries led to feelings of frustration from foreign merchants and delegates. Around 1868, one enterprising man tried an unusual scheme to force Korea into a trade agreement. His name was Ernst Oppert, and he was a Prussian merchant. Having been denied negotiations once by the Korean government, Oppert chose a new tactic: grave robbing. Encouraged by the French missionary Stanislas Ferón, Oppert and a crew of about one hundred Chinese and Malay pirates set sail aboard the steamer *China*. Their goal was to rob the royal tomb in Kayadong, or Gyeongsang, a southeastern province of present-day South Korea. Oppert and Ferón planned to steal the remains of Prince Namyon, father of the *taewon-gun* (Korea's prince regent). Even more tantalizing were rumors of gold buried within the vault. The two decided to steal the gold and hold the relics until the Korean government accepted Oppert's trade proposal.

However, Oppert's party underestimated the distance to Namyon's tomb. After a six-hour march and several hours of digging, the crew had not breached the vault. With low tide threatening to beach their vessel, Oppert and Ferón returned to their ship empty-handed. Still hopeful, Oppert sent a letter describing his trade proposals to the *taewon-gun*. The prince regent once again refused an agreement and threatened to destroy Oppert's ship. Oppert and his crew sailed from Korea with neither treaty nor gold.

at various times between 1866 and 1875. None of the major Western powers had managed to secure a trade agreement, and interest in Korea began to wane. The following year, the Japanese would succeed where others had failed.

Japanese diplomats arrived in 1869 and 1873 demanding trade rights. When the *taewon-gun* refused, Japanese ships attacked Korean soldiers at Kanghwa and the western port city of Inchon. During the attack, one Japanese ship was destroyed. In 1875, Japanese warships returned, demanding reparations for the loss of men and property during the attack. When peace talks mediated by China failed, four hundred Japanese troops arrived on Kanghwa, while another four thousand waited on nearby ships. Facing the threat of invasion, King Kojong agreed to Japan's demands. The conflict ended on February 27, 1876, with the signing of the Treaty of Kanghwa. The treaty gave Japan control over Korean trade and money lending, and a foothold in Korean government.

In a bid to limit Japanese power, the Korean and U.S. governments signed the Treaty of Amity and Commerce on May 22, 1882. The United States gained the rights to Korean ports and gave American traders rights identical to those awarded to Japanese traders. In addition, Korean and American citizens could purchase land within the allied countries. Korean scholars and students were also allowed entrance into American universities. A handful of Korean scholars took advantage of the provisions, journeying to America to attend prestigious universities such as Harvard and Princeton. In addition, the treaty promised,

perpetual peace and friendship between the President of the United States and the King of Chosen and the citizens and subjects of their respective governments. If another power deals unjustly or oppressively with either Government, the other will exert their good offices, on being informed of the case, to bring about an amicable arrangement, thus showing their friendly feelings.[2]

Deemed by the Koreans as the most valuable piece of the agreement, this item appeared to be a promise of American aid and protection in the event of foreign attack. The Korean government quickly signed treaties with Great Britain, Russia, France, and Italy to gain additional foreign protection.

Tonghak Rebellion

Not all Koreans viewed the foreign treaties as beneficial. The Korean economy relied on farming. The government earned income taxing farmers and selling crops. With the new trade agreements, foreign countries expected to buy goods from Korea at lower prices. These lower prices reduced government profits. Although the government made less money, it still spent the same amount. Before long, the Korean treasury was depleted, and the government needed to find new ways to make money. Because the aristocrats did not pay any taxes, the bulk of these costs fell to the peasants.

Millions of Koreans grew increasingly dissatisfied as they struggled to pay these taxes. They also faced starvation. Rather

These Korean officials are en route to the United States as part of a diplomatic mission in 1871.

than keep rice and grain at home to feed the peasantry, the government continued to sell farm goods overseas for profit. Many lower-class Koreans faced rising grain prices and food shortages. Poverty became widespread. Droughts in 1876 and 1877 and again ten years later further weakened the Korean treasury. One Korean recalled the droughts: "We had nothing to eat. There was absolutely no way we could survive."[3]

Although farming revenue dropped, government expenses did not. To cover the decrease in funds, officials implemented even more taxation. Peasants applied for loans to pay the taxes, but when the payments were not met, the people lost their lands and homes. Farmers and miners flooded into the cities looking for

jobs, but few opportunities remained. Foreign investors had purchased rights to mines, fishing ports, and other businesses, employing their countrymen instead of Koreans.

Many Koreans blamed foreigners for their poverty, and movements arose demanding an end to foreign involvement. The largest movement was the *Tonghak*, or Eastern Learning. Founded by Ch'oe Che-u in the 1860s, *Tonghak* combined Buddhism, Confucianism, and Taoism. Ch'oe preached the equality of all people, an appealing idea to the disgruntled farmers and lower classes. The motto of the movement was, "Drive out the Japanese dwarfs and the Western barbarians, and praise righteousness."[4]

Inspired by Ch'oe's teachings, the *Tonghak* followers rebelled in 1892. The leaders spread leaflets and marched on palaces and towns to call for social reform. One leaflet protested how the aristocrats lived well while the peasantry starved:

The people are the root of the nation. If the root withers, the nation will be enfeebled. Heedless of their responsibility for sustaining the state and providing for its people, the officials build lavish residences in the countryside. . . . We are wretched village people far from the capital, yet we feed and clothe ourselves with the bounty of the sovereign's land. We cannot sit by and watch our nation perish. The whole nation is as one, its multitudes united in their determination to raise the righteous standard of revolt.[5]

King Kojong ordered the rebel leaders back to their homes. Several thousand *Tonghak* supporters later assembled to demand government reform, expulsion of Christians, Japanese, and Westerners, and the dissolution of all foreign treaties. When his commands to stop the move-

Founder of the Tonghak *movement, Ch'oe Che-u advocated the equality of all people.*

ment were ignored, King Kojong sent a force of eight hundred soldiers to meet the estimated twenty thousand rebels. The rebels defeated the soldiers, and the flame of *Tonghak* soon swept across Korea.

Japanese Annexation

King Kojong appealed to China for aid in suppressing the rebellion, and China sent troops to assist. Japan viewed the presence of Chinese troops as a violation of a previous treaty. Battles between Japan and China broke out on Korean soil in 1894. These military conflicts caused significant loss of Korean property and life. The Korean king pleaded with his neighbors not to carry their disputes into his kingdom, but he was ignored. After Japan defeated China, the Japanese emperor demanded the Chinese withdraw from Korean politics. The Japanese victory resulted in increased Japanese influence in Korea.

The Koreans would not submit quietly. Approximately seventy thousand guerrilla warriors fought nearly fifteen hundred battles against the Japanese occupiers between 1907 and 1910. Organized into small units, the Japanese military easily defeated the pockets of rebels. By 1910, most rebels had fled the country, and the Japanese were in control of Korea.

The Japanese Empire was no longer content to call Korea a protectorate, or partially controlled country. Determined to gain complete control of the kingdom, on August 29, 1910, Japanese diplomats forced King Kojong to abdicate in favor of his son, Sunjong. However, Prince Sunjong was young, and one source indicates

Japanese firing squads executed thousands of March First revolutionaries for attempting to overthrow Japanese control of Korea.

he may have been developmentally disabled. The Japanese government created a cabinet to oversee Sunjong's rule, and Japanese officials were placed in each government office. With the Japanese in charge of the military and treasury, the weak young king could not protest. With its people already in control of the government, the Japanese Empire easily took control of Korea.

Japanese Reforms

Most Western powers thought that Japanese rule of Korea was a good thing. The Japanese Empire had adopted a number of Western customs and trade partners, and was considered civilized by most Western governments. When Japan enacted a series of reforms in Korea, Western governments considered the changes progressive. One of the first acts was the outlawing of the topknot. For Korean men, this unique

hairstyle indicated entrance into manhood. Cutting off the topknot was viewed as an insult against one's father and family. According to Bong-Youn Choy in *Koreans in America*, "Outlawing this age-old social custom meant national humiliation."[6] One father even committed suicide after learning his sons had cut off their topknots.

The Japanese government also installed its own citizens in influential positions. The Japanese received higher wages and government positions previously reserved for the *yangban*. From government administrators to school principals, thousands of Korean jobs were given to the Japanese. This move aggravated the already bleak financial situation of many Koreans.

The Japanese also required Koreans to prove land ownership. When documents were not produced, the Japanese took possession of Korean farms and property. Land that had been farmed by the same family for generations was handed over to the occupiers. Over 21.9 million acres were confiscated and given to Japanese colonists. One Japanese company owned 20 percent of Korea's tillable land and determined what would be farmed or built on the property.

The empire moved to eradicate all Korean language, customs, and symbols. Koreans were no longer to display the Korean flag in their homes. In schools, children learned to speak Japanese, and all communication in *hangul*, the Korean alphabet, was outlawed. Japanese soldiers conducted raids on homes, confiscating and burning any documents written in the native language. Koreans were prohibited from public speeches and meetings. A Korean immigrant described the conditions under Japanese control: "Oh, it was a hard time. . . . Under the Japanese, no freedom. Not even free talking."[7]

For many, the final blow came when the emperor forced Koreans to adopt Japanese names. Korean names are very symbolic. Factors such as the day, month, hour, and year a person is born are considered when creating a name. The loss of one's name meant the loss of personal identity. Those who refused to take a Japanese name were punished, by either imprisonment or execution. If a person fled, any remaining family members were punished in his or her place.

Christians received some of the harshest punishments as a result of the reforms. Reports claimed Japanese soldiers burned Christian churches to the ground with the parishioners trapped inside. Mary Paik Lee recalled Japanese soldiers murdering Christian Koreans in her autobiography, *Quiet Odyssey*: "The Japanese soldiers had rounded up as many men as they could find, had herded them into a church

Korean schoolchildren write Japanese characters. Under Japanese rule, they were forbidden from speaking and writing in Korean.

Stolen Identities

For athletes, winning an Olympic medal represents the fulfillment of a lifelong dream, a chance to honor their countries and have their names recorded among the world's greatest athletes. During the Japanese occupation, two Korean runners who participated in the 1936 Berlin Olympics were forced to give up their identities. Their names were Sohn Kee-chung and Nam Sung-yong. Both men qualified for the marathon at the Olympic trials in Tokyo, much to the dismay of the Japanese government, which only wanted Japanese runners to compete. The Japanese government agreed to send Sohn and Nam to Berlin, but only as Japanese subjects with Japanese names. Sohn became "Kitei Son," and Nam was "Shoryu Nan."

With his time of 2:29:19, Sohn won the gold and set a new world record. His teammate Nam was close behind at 2:31:42, taking home the bronze. They accepted their awards with bowed heads as the Japanese anthem played. Although Sohn tried to explain to reporters he was Korean, the Japanese blocked his statements. In protest, the staff of Korea's *Dong-A Ilbo* newspaper removed the Japanese flag from Sohn's uniform in his victory photo. The newspaper was raided and several members of the staff were arrested or imprisoned.

For over sixty years, Sohn petitioned the Olympic committee to officially recognize the Korean champions' true names. In 1986, a monument in Culver City, California, became the first Olympic memorial to display the names of Nam and Sohn. Sohn died in 2000 and Nam the following year, their greatest dream still unrealized. As of 2004, the official Olympic Web site still listed the Koreans by their Japanese names.

and shot them to death."[8] An estimated two hundred thousand rebellion-minded Koreans were arrested and tortured during Japanese rule.

The goal of the Japanese was to stamp out any native Korean customs and beliefs. By replacing Korean ideas with their own, the Japanese believed Koreans would become just like any other Japanese citizens. For the Koreans, the changes meant loss of identity and their national pride. They wanted to be Korean, not Japanese.

Rebellion

While Japanese and Western powers considered these reforms progressive, the Koreans viewed the changes as the extermination of their cultural identity. Koreans used a number of methods to voice their dissatisfaction with Japanese control. Provincial farmers refused to plant and tend their crops. The lack of supply led to food shortages and skyrocketing prices in major population centers like Seoul.

Others organized peaceful marches to protest the Japanese occupancy. One such exhibition was the March First movement of 1919. Thirty-three scholars and their supporters distributed Korean flags and declared their independence from Japan. More than five hundred thousand Koreans in six hundred locations voiced their support. The Japanese responded with violence. An estimated seventy-five hundred Koreans were killed and forty-five thousand were arrested for demanding their freedom.

Patriots who managed to escape Japanese persecution fled to Manchuria and other countries. Myung-ja Sur, a participant in the movement, described the March First aftermath: "Because the Japanese oppression was so severe for all Koreans, especially Korean patriots, I had to flee to Shanghai. The Japanese went crazy. They beat up and killed thousands of Koreans while many were arrested and later killed."[9]

A New Life

Decades of war and oppression left many Koreans hungry, homeless, and impoverished. Under Japanese rule, there was little hope for advancement or monetary success, even for the cultural elite—the most desirable property and jobs were awarded to the Japanese.

These Korean women were forced to serve as sex slaves to Japanese soldiers during World War II.

Faced with continued oppression, the Koreans had only two options: accept Japan or build a new life elsewhere.

While Korea was in a state of turmoil, new opportunities arose in America. Under their treaty with the United States, Koreans were given rights to land and citizenship. With their prospects for a good life in Korea waning, some Koreans began to flee to America for survival. Many of these emigrants were scholars and ministers facing religious or political persecution. Others were poor laborers robbed of their land and left destitute by high taxes. Each carried with them the traditions of their homeland and a spirit determined to succeed in the new land.

CHAPTER TWO

A New Beginning

Prior to 1900, the number of Koreans in America was almost negligible: only about twenty Koreans living in Hawaii, mainly employed as ginseng merchants. A handful of scholars also arrived to study in American universities as part of the Chemulpo Treaty signed by Korea and the United States in 1882. However, once the United States gained control of the Hawaiian Islands, opportunities arose for more Koreans to immigrate to America.

Involved for decades in the affairs of Hawaii, the United States expanded its territory by formally annexing the Kingdom of Hawaii on July 7, 1898. Initially interested in using Hawaii as a military post in the Pacific, the United States soon took interest in Hawaii's profitable sugar industry. Thousands of jobs became available to Americans on Hawaii's sugar plantations. However, European immigrants from America were expensive to import, demanded higher wages and better services, and could not be persuaded to work as plantation labor. Faced with a labor shortage, U.S. officials and plantation owners hired Chinese and Japanese laborers to meet the need for cheap labor. These two groups became Hawaii's dominant workforce for decades.

By the late 1800s, U.S. legislation reacted to growing anti-Chinese sentiment

Americans, the Chinese could no longer be imported, and the Japanese workforce was becoming more powerful and difficult to manage. Plantation owners determined they needed another labor source to supplement the decrease in Chinese immigrants and provide competition for the Japanese. Korea became the answer to the sugar planters' problems.

Workers for Hire

One of the most influential supporters of Korean immigration was an American named Horace Allen. Allen first arrived in Korea as a missionary in 1876. He became a close friend of the royal family after saving the life of Queen Min's nephew, Min Yongik, during a failed coup. Allen's close relationship with the king and queen led to many diplomatic appointments, including his eventual position as American foreign minister to Korea. Allen had already proved his worth by securing Korean gold mining interests for American businessmen, and Hawaiian planters hoped he would do the same for the sugar industry.

In 1902, Allen met with members of the Hawaiian Sugar Planters' Association (HSPA) and provided a favorable account of the Korean people. Allen described Koreans as a "docile, good-natured, patient and hard-working race." He also went on to say, "Ages of subjection to their superi-

This young girl is one of thousands of Korean immigrants who came to Hawaii to work in the sugarcane fields.

among the public and prohibited the entrance of additional Chinese workers to meet the growing need for plantation laborers. As the Japanese workforce became more dominant, they demanded improved wages and working conditions. Japanese workers organized a series of strikes and work stoppages to protest plantation conditions.

Needing to increase their current labor population, plantation owners found themselves in a difficult position. The plantations did not pay enough to lure European ors make them law abiding and easy to govern; at the same time they seem able to absorb ideas of liberty and equality very readily."[10]

In addition to his recommendation, Allen also promised to gain immigration approval from King Kojong and his government, acting on behalf of the planters in Washington, D.C. As part of his promise, Allen appointed his friend, David Deshler, as a recruiter in Korea.

Recruitment

Deshler established the East-West Development Company to secure Korean laborers. He set up offices in Inchon and other port cities, and hired Koreans to work as recruiters and interpreters. Deshler placed ads in Korean newspapers and traveled to various ports, hoping to attract laborers. As part of his campaign to lure Koreans to Hawaii, Deshler posted enticing descriptions exaggerating the climate and working conditions on the plantations. One such advertisement read:

> The climate is suitable for everyone and there is no severe heat or cold. There are schools on every island. English is taught and the tuition is free. Jobs for the farmers are available all the year round for those who are healthy and decent in behavior. Monthly payment is fifteen dollars in American money (sixty-seven won in Korean money). There are ten hours of work a day with Sunday free. The expenses for housing, fuel, water, and hospital will be paid by the employer.[11]

At first, few Koreans expressed interest. Ancestor worship was part of the Confucian tradition, and many Koreans viewed leaving Korea as abandoning the memories of their forebears. However, as conditions in Korea worsened, Deshler's offer became more appealing. Weary of poverty and oppression, many Koreans took advantage of the opportunity and agreed to make the voyage to Hawaii.

Deshler's Bank

Prior to 1885, many immigrants arriving in the United States came as indentured

In the late 1800s, American missionary Horace Allen encouraged Korean immigration to the United States.

Although Korean Christians were able to worship in the safety of American missions like this one in Seoul, Christianity was officially outlawed during the Japanese occupation.

servants. Employers paid for passage in exchange for a period (usually seven years) of unpaid labor. Under this practice, individuals could immigrate without money, and their sponsors gained profits from the free labor. In 1885, the U.S. government declared indentured servitude unethical, and the practice became illegal. Businesses could no longer provide transport fees and faced penalties for hiring laborers before their arrival in the United States. Potential immigrants were also left with no means to pay for their voyage.

In 1902, the average cost of a passage from Korea to Hawaii was one hundred dollars. Fifty dollars covered physical examinations, steamship passage, and passports, while the other half was required to cover living expenses in Hawaii. The United States government required immigrants to bring the additional fifty dollars as proof they could survive on their own and would not look to the government for assistance after they reached Hawaii. For potential Korean immigrants, the sum was an impossible amount.

To overcome this obstacle, Allen and the HSPA created banks in both Korea and Hawaii. Funded by money from the planters and overseen by David Deshler, the banks loaned Koreans the necessary one hundred dollars—fifty for steamship passage and a fifty-dollar banknote to show immigration officials proof they could meet the fifty-dollar personal requirement. Once the immigrants passed through immigration, they returned the notes to the bank office in Hawaii. The immigrants received no money in exchange for the note but were at least guaranteed passage through immigration. Although technically a violation of U.S. immigration law, the HSPA received assurances from Allen that he would prevent the government from detecting their actions.

Missionary Influence

Deshler's recruiters were not the only ones preaching the benefits of immigration. American missionaries had a tremendous impact on the immigration of Christian Koreans. Under the Japanese occupation, Christians were not free to worship. So, the missionaries working in Korea spoke often of the religious and political freedom offered in America and urged their parishioners to move to Hawaii. Missionaries described Hawaii as a paradise, tantalizing Koreans with tales of a country where clothing was said to grow on trees and a fortune in gold, free for the taking, lay in rivers.

Missionaries also told their followers evangelism was their duty and asked them to take the religion to the islands. One missionary, the Reverend George Heber Jones, is credited with persuading between fifty and seventy of the first immigrants to make the journey. Jones is reported to have remarked to his congregation that "the weather and scenery in Hawaii were very agreeable and furthermore, as Christians, they could set up a church there and evangelize."[12] Encouraged by their religious leaders and expecting easy work and a temperate environment, the first Koreans decided to make the journey to America.

Voyage to America

As word spread of Hawaii's opportunities, port cities like Inchon became packed with Koreans eager to come to America. Men and women sold their homes and property in preparation for the trip. After visiting Deshler's bank, immigrants waited for a ship. As the number of immigrants grew, temporary living quarters were erected to house them while they waited. The accommodations were meager, often little more than hastily erected wooden barracks. The first two voyages to America were approximately one month apart, but subsequent journeys were made anywhere from two weeks to a few days apart.

When enough fares were collected, the ships were loaded. The steamers first sailed to Japan. Here, immigrants were given a series of physical exams to determine if they were fit for plantation work. After the physicals, approved applicants were again assigned to temporary housing while they awaited the next ship bound for Hawaii.

Once on board, men and women were packed together into stifling, dimly lit steerage holds beneath the ship's decks. Gender separation was an ancient Korean custom; even in the home men and women stayed in different rooms. On the ship, they all roomed together, and the arrangement was awkward and uncomfortable. The immigrants slept on hard, narrow wooden bunks. All their daily functions—eating, sleeping, and relieving themselves—were conducted in the holds. Before long, the rooms reeked of urine, sweat, and excrement.

The voyage from Japan to Honolulu lasted between ten and twenty days. The ships frequently encountered storms, and sailing was often rough. Most of the passengers were overcome with seasickness and struggled to keep down their meager rations of rice and fish. One immigrant later shared his experience: "The boat was now rolling so violently, tossing around all the moveable things in it from side to side. I was one of them. It made me very sick, indeed, and it made everyone else sick."[13]

When they finally arrived in Hawaii, the immigrants were kept on the ships to endure yet another set of physical exams. Despite the earlier rounds of exams, some Koreans were still turned away. The poor conditions on the ships resulted in frequent illness among the passengers, and many who had been healthy when they left Korea were unfit for work once they arrived in Hawaii and were forced to return to their homeland. Those who passed the physicals were taken by train or boat to one of the plantations.

The first wave of 83 Korean immigrants arrived on January 13, 1903, on board the USS *Gaelic*. While 102 originally left Korea, 19 were turned away after they failed to pass their physicals. Over the next two years, about 8,000 Koreans successfully entered the United States on sixty-five ships.

Social Hierarchy on the Plantations

When Korean workers arrived on the plantations, they discovered they had exchanged one social hierarchy for another, and once again their names were stolen. Laborers received a bronze disk called a *pŏnhos*, each engraved with a number. Workers were called by their numbers instead of by their names. Koreans escaping Japanese oppression were outraged to discover their identities once again denied.

They also found themselves at the bottom of the social pyramid. In addition to the owners, each plantation had several managers, overseers, and foremen. The managers were in charge of the day-to-day functioning of the plantation. Below them were the foremen, who were responsible for different segments of the business, such as accounting, purchasing, and production. Overseers were responsible for the workers in the field. One overseer supervised as many as fifty laborers. Often these large teams were separated into divisions of twenty workers and were overseen by foremen called *lunas*.

Most *lunas* were white, and their cruelty toward the laborers was legendary. Beatings and verbal abuse became common. One woman recalled her mother sleeping through the morning call to work and forgetting to wake the rest of the family: "We were all asleep—my brother and his wife, my older sister, and myself. Suddenly, the door swung open, and a big burly *luna* burst in, screaming and cursing, 'Get up, get to work.' The *luna* ran around the room, ripping off the covers, not caring whether my family was dressed or not."[14]

Plantation Work

Expecting streets paved with gold, many new immigrants found life on the plantation worse than in Korea. The immigrants worked six days a week in the sugarcane fields, planting and weeding the cane. In addition to planting and weeding, workers stripped the razor-sharp leaves and cut twelve-foot-long canes. Their hands became covered with blisters and cuts.

An average day for a plantation worker lasted ten hours, sometimes longer during the harvest season. They awoke before dawn and worked until five o'clock in the evening. Anna Choi recalled her work in the fields:

It was very hard work for me. I arose at four o'clock in the morning and we took a truck to the sugarcane fields, eating breakfast along the way. Work in the sugar plantation was back-breaking. It involved cutting sugarcanes, watering, and pulling out weeds. All the work at that time was accomplished with manpower, for tractors and farming machinery were not in use like they are today. The sugarcane fields were endless and twice the height of myself.[15]

Laborers were considered commodities, not people. The conditions were brutal,

Plantation Life

See Hong-Ki was one of the earliest Korean immigrants to arrive in Hawaii. He came to the islands in 1903. In Bong-Youn Choy's book Koreans in America, *See describes his life on the Kolora plantation:*

I got up at four-thirty in the morning and made my breakfast: I had to be out to the field at five o'clock and work started at five-thirty. I quit work at four-thirty in the afternoon and had a half an hour for lunch. I worked ten hours a day with a sixty-seven cents a day wage. . . . The supervisor or foreman was called *luna* in Hawaiian language and my *luna* was German. He was very strict with us. . . . He did not allow us to smoke and did not allow us to stand up straight once we started to work. He treated us like cows and horses. If any one violated his orders, he was punished, usually a slap on the face or flagellating without mercy. We couldn't protest against the *luna*'s treatment because we were in fear that we would be fired. . . . We carried our number all the time as an identification card, and we were never called by name, but number. I lived in the camp: it was just like the army barracks; wooden floors and we slept on wooden beds or just on the floor, with one blanket over the body. Usually four single men lived in one room. . . . Sometimes I could not sleep at all due to the hot air.

with the laborers often working in one-hundred-degree heat under heavy humidity. The immigrants suffered heat exhaustion and sunburn. Although they worked with other Koreans, conversation between workers was forbidden. Physical violence was common on the plantations, with the supervisors beating those who talked, smoked, or disobeyed plantation rules. Yang Choo-en was one of the first Koreans in Hawaii. In an interview with Bong-Youn Choy, he remembers life on the plantation. "We worked like draft animals, cows and horses in the plantation fields, and we were treated like animals by the *lunas* or foremen during work, even not allowing us to talk or smoke with each other."[16]

Another woman remembered a supervisor using a whip on the laborers. "I'll never forget the foreman. He said we work like 'lazy.' He wanted us to work faster. He would gallop around on horseback and crack and snap his whip."[17]

At the end of the workday, laborers returned to the camps for meals. Exhausted, most of the workers immediately went to bed. After a long day in the fields, there was little time for leisure activities. Men who did have spare time generally engaged in drinking and gambling. On Sundays, the workers were allowed time off to attend worship services.

Camp Conditions

Plantation housing structures mimicked the social hierarchy. While the owners basked in wealth and luxury, the homes of the workers were quite different. Below the owners' sprawling mansions were the tidy, attractive bungalows given to the managers and overseers. At the very bottom were the shacks and barracks assigned to the laborers.

The primitive living arrangements lacked comfort and privacy. Single men

Immigrant laborers on Hawaii's sugarcane plantations lived in cramped and unsanitary conditions in barracks like this one.

lived together in one barrack, and the living quarters were usually segregated based on nationality. Japanese, Chinese—and later Filipino—workers were all housed separately from Korean laborers. When barracks were not available, four men were assigned to share a small shack. If a man had a family, he might be given a room in the barracks or occasionally a small house. Meals were eaten as a group in a large kitchen facility, and these were usually segregated as well.

One worker remarked that the sewage was even stratified. The pipes started near the owner's home and flowed down the hill toward the field-workers' shacks, leaving the low tiers awash in filth. By the time it reached the bottom, the smell was unbearable. The unsanitary conditions led to disease and often death. An inspector once described the camps as "decrepit and dilapidated rookeries with roofs leaking and danger and disease threatening the occupants, with masses of filth blocking the drains and decaying refuse all about and beneath the houses."[18]

Although health care was provided on the plantations, language barriers prevented patients from accurately describing their symptoms to doctors. Many immigrants died as the result of inadequate health care. Yang Choo-en recalled watching other workers succumb to the wretched conditions of the plantation: "I saw with my own eyes some of my good friends die in the plantation camps. In fact, one of them died in my lap with an unknown illness after he got back from his doctor."[19]

On some plantations, workers were not charged for living in the barracks. On others, they were expected to pay for accommodations. Workers paid for their own meals, with monthly fees averaging about six dollars. There were also charges for additional services such as laundry. The immigrants made only sixteen dollars each month, and these extra fees quickly drained the immigrants' already meager resources. Most of these costs went directly into the plantation owners' pockets, leaving very little for the Koreans themselves.

While many Korean immigrants desired to return home, few had the means to do so. Low wages prevented any hope of saving enough money for a return trip, and the laborers felt trapped. With no other options, they endured the harsh plantation work and hoped for new opportunities.

Japanese Intervention

Traditionally, a country with an immigrant population in the United States supplied a representative to monitor the immigrants and ensure that the people were well treated in their new jobs. King Kojong failed to appoint a representative, despite numerous suggestions by the U.S. government. As a result, there was no one to look after the interests of the Korean workers. The plantation owners were able to treat the Koreans poorly, and there was no one to defend them.

By 1905, Japan had gained influence over Korea, and the flow of Korean labor began to dwindle. Hearing rumors of poor conditions, the Japanese appointed officials to investigate the plantations. The confirmed reports shocked the Japanese

Rats and Snakes

Housing conditions for immigrants were very poor. In addition to being small and cramped, housing was often dirty and infested with parasites. In her autobiography, Quiet Odyssey, *author Mary Paik Lee describes how she and her siblings encountered animals in their beds:*

As I stretched my legs on my shelf bed, I felt a cold, rough object against my toes. I threw back the blanket and saw a red snake coiled up. It was as surprised as I was and slithered off outside. After that, we always pounded our beds with a long stick before jumping in. Then I woke up one night feeling a sharp pain on my nose and found myself staring at two black, beady eyes. I screamed. Father came running to see what was wrong. A big rat about the size of a baby kitten had tried to eat my nose. No wonder the cat was afraid of the rats.

government. Arguing that the Korean workers were treated no better than slaves, the Japanese refused to allow additional Korean workers to enter Hawaii, and Japanese officials denied passports to emigrants.

The Korean American population argued against Japanese involvement. The majority of Koreans believed the Japanese did not truly have their best interests at heart and claimed they were not responding to poor plantation conditions but rather to complaints from Japanese laborers about stiff job competition from Koreans. Regardless of their complaints, the Japanese halted Korean immigration after only two years.

Picture Brides

The immigration ban had some exceptions. At the time that immigration ceased, 80 percent of the seven thousand immigrants were male. Korean women were a rarity in the United States. For the Korean men in Hawaii, the lack of females presented an uncomfortable problem. As the immigrant population grew older, many Korean men desired to start families. The immigration stoppage meant no wives were available for these men.

The Japanese and American governments did allow one concession to the immigration laws. Called the Gentlemen's Agreement, the law allowed unmarried Korean women to enter the United States for the purpose of marriage.

But many Korean men could not afford to go home and meet a wife. To solve this dilemma, Korean Americans adopted the picture bride system. Korean men sent photos of themselves to matchmakers in the homeland. After consulting with a matchmaker, eligible women viewed the photos and selected their mate based on his appearance.

The first Korean picture bride was Sara Choe, who arrived in Hawaii on November 28, 1910, as the bride of Lee Nai-soo. Between 1910 and 1924, over eight hundred brides arrived in Hawaii.

Korean matchmakers sent women known as picture brides to marry Korean men in the United States.

Women on the Plantations

For Korean women, the voyage to America was quite different from what they had imagined. In Korea, women rarely worked outside the home and were occupied with traditional tasks like housekeeping and child rearing. Most women expected their positions to be the same in Hawaii. Some of the picture brides were even better educated or of higher social status than their husbands and had grown accustomed to servants. Once they arrived in Hawaii, the new brides discovered they could not raise families on their husbands' income, and their responsibilities changed.

While they were not required to work, some Korean women found jobs on the plantation to help make ends meet. Many worked as cooks, helping to prepare food for the laborers. One Korean immigrant remembered a neighbor woman earning money cooking for several men:

> On the Honokaa Plantation, Mrs. Tai Yoo Kim prepared meals for her husband and twenty bachelors. Every morning at five o'clock, she fed them a breakfast of rice, broth, and *kimchi* [spicy pickled vegetables, usually cabbage]. For six days a week, she packed twenty-one lunch tins with rice and dried salt fish. Then for dinner she prepared soup, rice, and a soy-seasoned dish of vegetables, meat, or fish, or a dish of corned beef and onions.[20]

Other women assisted in laundries, charging bachelors small fees for cleaning and mending their clothing. One Korean woman recalled: "I made custom shirts with handbound button holes for 25 cents. My mother and sister-in-law took in laundry. They scrubbed, ironed and mended shirts for a nickel a piece. It was pitiful! Their knuckles became swollen and raw from using the harsh yellow soap."[21]

Some even worked in the plantation fields with the men, weeding and cultivating the sugar crop. One woman noted the vast difference in her mother's life in Korea compared to in Hawaii: "My mother had many maids in Korea, but at Kipahulu plantation she worked in the canefields with my older brother and his wife. I remember her hands, so blistered and raw that she had to wrap them in clothes."[22] Although they worked the same hours and performed the same tasks as the men, Korean women received lower wages. The average pay for a female worker was twelve dollars a month.

The female presence was the most important factor in the early days of immigration. As Korean men gained wives and families, they sought to move away from the harsh plantation environment. They desired greater opportunities for their children beyond lives as field laborers. Hearing of higher wages and greater opportunities in California and other western states, many Korean Americans left the plantations for the mainland.

CHAPTER THREE

The Mainland and Discrimination

As the United States population continued to grow, more services were created, including railroads. Lured by the higher wages offered by rail companies, many Koreans moved from Hawaii to the mainland. Once again, the immigrants expected gold-lined streets, and once again they met with disappointment.

Difficult working conditions were not the only challenges awaiting Koreans in America. After leaving Hawaii, many Korean Americans struggled to adapt to life on the mainland. While Asians were acceptable as plantation labor, Euro-Americans resented the growing Asian presence in the continental United States. Many thought the Koreans were violating their work agreements by leaving Hawaii. The new immigrants found themselves at odds with European Americans as they both competed for the same jobs.

While most of the backlash was aimed at the Chinese and Japanese, cultural ignorance prevented white Americans from discerning between the different Asian groups. Koreans quickly became targets for discrimination. The new opportunities promised by the mainland quickly disintegrated.

Moving to the Mainland

As soon as they could afford the passage, Koreans moved to the mainland, settling mostly in California, Oregon, Washington, Utah, and Montana. Approximately one thousand Korean immigrants entered California between 1904 and 1907. California offered a variety of occupations, including work for railroads, mines, and farms. Many Koreans found jobs as fruit pickers in California's citrus groves.

Immigrants found the conditions were not much different from that on the plantations. The accommodations were still primitive, with the workers and their families living in tiny camps. The working hours were long, and the tasks continued to be physically demanding. The temperatures were almost as hot as those in Hawaii. One Korean immigrant recalled the high temperatures in California: "The day starts out around seventy to eighty degrees and by noon time the temperature reaches around a hundred and five and a hundred and ten degrees."[23]

The orchards presented other hazards, including insects and venomous spiders. One Korean American recalled his experiences in the orchards:

If you picked grapes you had to be careful where you put your hand in the vines because black widow spiders and yellow-jacket hornets were all over the grapevines. Yellow-jackets built their nests so that they were difficult to find and black widows wove their spider webs all over the vine. As soon as I was stung by yellow-jackets I used to make mud-packs and place them on the wound to prevent the bite from swelling.[24]

Yellow Peril

In addition to the poor overall working conditions, the Korean Americans met with a new challenge in California: greater racial discrimination. On the Hawaiian plantations, Koreans and other workers were separated from most European Americans. The only Caucasians they might see were employed at the plantation, and there was little opportunity for Koreans to mingle with other Americans. On the mainland, however, it was a different story, and the Koreans were unprepared for the discrimination they encountered.

As the numbers of Koreans and other Asian immigrants increased, concerns grew among European Americans over competition for menial jobs, such as laborers and miners. The Korean immigrants were willing to work longer hours and for lower wages than Caucasians, prompting employers to hire them over European American workers. Resentment from European Americans increased through the belief that soon Koreans and other Asians would win all job opportunities. Termed the "Yellow Peril," the fear of Asian workers was strongest in California, where Korean and other Asian populations were largest. Korean immigrants met with hostility when they arrived on the mainland.

Many Korean Americans in professional fields had difficulty finding work. Jobs were not as plentiful as they expected, and many found themselves passed over in favor of Caucasian work-

Riverside 1912

Willing to work long hours for low wages, Korean immigrants like these orchard workers in Riverside, California, faced hostility from many European American immigrants.

ers. The community distrust prevented Caucasian Americans from visiting Korean professionals, such as doctors and attorneys. Although the Koreans were educated and trained professionals, European Americans would not seek their services. With few clients, well-educated Korean men, formerly the most respected members of their society, abandoned their professions to avoid starvation. These scholars and professionals accepted menial jobs as janitors, houseboys, and laborers to earn money to support their families.

Those who imagined America as a land of freedom and opportunity were bitterly disappointed. In Ronald Takaki's book *Strangers from a Different Shore*, Whang Sa Sun describes his experience trying to find a job: "I felt the discrimination and realized that America was not a free country. Everybody did not enjoy liberty. The American people saw the Asian people as a different race. They didn't respect the Asian people. I wanted some postal or factory work, but they didn't give it to me. I couldn't get a job."[25]

Cultural misunderstanding further fueled racism toward Korean immigrants. To many Caucasians, a Korean was not discernible from a Chinese or Japanese, and racial bias against those two cultures spilled over to Korean immigrants. Physical differences made Korean immigrants easy targets for angry Caucasians. In addition, many Koreans maintained cultural ties, wearing traditional clothing and continuing to speak their native language. A lack of understanding stirred up resentment and fear of these newcomers.

Separate Facilities

As racial fears increased, European Americans made their communities inhospitable to Koreans to prevent immigrants from settling in their areas. Businesses adopted "white only" policies and refused to trade with Koreans. Koreans also experienced difficulties acquiring adequate housing. Landlords refused to rent or sell homes to Koreans. Those willing to rent to Koreans usually offered substandard housing in the city's slums, charging tenants enormous rates for small, dirty facilities. Mary Paik Lee describes her family's Riverside, California, home in her autobiography, *Quiet Odyssey:* "There was no pretense of making it livable—just four walls, one window, and one door—nothing else. We put mud in the cracks to keep the wind out. The water pump served several shacks. We had to heat our bath water in a bucket over an open fire outside, then pour it into a tin tub inside. There was no gas or electricity."[26]

In *Strangers from a Different Shore*, Do-yun Yoon remarks on the challenges of trying to find housing: "In renting a place only the 'junk house' was available. None in the nice areas in the 'white town,' Only in 'Mexican town' or 'Black town.'"[27]

Although they desired better housing, Korean Americans had

few options. In addition to houses, landowners also denied Koreans leases and mortgages for undeveloped land. Unable to build their own homes, Koreans were forced to accept the conditions or move to a new area, which would often prove just as unfriendly.

In some communities, Koreans were denied access to community facilities, such as movie theaters, swimming pools, restaurants, and hotels. While some facilities did offer minority facilities, in others the Koreans were forced to do without. Do-yun Yoon remembers trying to see a movie in California: "When we first came to Delano, the Americans would not let us sit anywhere in the theater. They permit-

Korean immigrants who wore traditional dress and spoke in their native language were frequent targets of xenophobia.

ted us to sit in one corner with the Mexicans but not the Americans."[28]

Another immigrant was refused service in a restaurant because the owners were afraid Caucasian customers would no longer go there if the business was seen catering to Asians. He said:

I entered a restaurant and sat down in order to have lunch. Although there were not many customers, the waitress did not come to my table. After awhile, a young receptionist came to me and said with a low voice that, "we can't serve you lunch, because if we start serving lunch to Orientals, white Americans will not come here."[29]

Even Korean children were affected by the pervasive fear of Asian Americans. In many towns, Korean children were prohibited from attending schools. For example, in 1906 the San Francisco school board determined that Korean and other Asian children, although born in America, could not attend the same schools as white children. It was decreed that these children would attend a special "Oriental School" instead, so as not to mingle with white children.

Physical Violence

In some areas, the fear of Korean immigrants became so great that white citizens took drastic, even violent, measures to deter Korean immigrants from settling near their cities. Organizations such as the Japanese and Korean Exclusion League were formed to drive Koreans out of towns and to propose measures limiting the freedoms of Korean Americans. Immigrants were pelted with rocks as they walked down the streets. In some towns, Korean homes and businesses were destroyed to force out the immigrants.

Easurk Emsen Charr was ten years old when he immigrated to the United States. In his autobiography, *The Golden Mountain*, Charr remembers attending a church service in California when someone threw a rock through the window: "It was just when we all stood up and were singing the closing hymn, a well-aimed missile, a fist-sized rock, like a bombshell, banged through the front window, barely missing Brother Pang and me."[30]

Korean Americans also faced racial slurs. They were often called "chinks" or "Japs" from racist European Americans who did not understand that Koreans were a different people. Mary Paik Lee recalls being taunted by schoolmates on her first day in an American school in her book, *Quiet Odyssey:* "As we entered the schoolyard, several girls formed a ring around us, singing a song and dancing in a circle. When they stopped, each one came over to me and hit me in the neck, hurting and frightening me."[31] Lee later discovered the lyrics of the song:

Ching Chong, Chinaman

Sitting on a wall.

Along came a white man,

And chopped his head off.[32]

In his autobiography, Easurk Emsen Charr chronicles the persecution he faced as a Korean American growing up in California.

Violence toward Korean Americans escalated from rocks and harsh words. Organizations like the Japanese and Korean Exclusion League were formed by white workers to protest the arrival of Korean workers. In the orchards and groves of California, mobs of white workers destroyed and burned Korean settlements. In June 1913, hundreds of angry European Americans confronted fifteen Koreans outside a railway station near Hemet, California. The Koreans had been hired to work as fruit pickers. The mob threatened the Koreans, stating that harm would come to any who left the train to go to their jobs. Frightened for their lives, the Koreans decided to remain on the train,

losing their jobs but possibly saving their lives.

In the most famous incident, Mrs. Mary Steward armed her Korean workers with guns after repeated raids by angry neighbors. In an ironic twist, many of Steward's neighbors began hiring Koreans themselves once Steward started recommending her workers to others.

As the violence escalated, Korean Americans turned to the American government for protection. Their pleas fell on deaf ears. Because Koreans did not qualify for citizenship and could not vote, lawmakers felt no obligation to protect their interests. Discrimination continued to blossom unchecked.

Alien Land Act

Rather than address the growing violence and discrimination, state and local governments restructured immigration laws. This series of laws was aimed at excluding Koreans and other Asian Americans from gaining wealth and prosperity. One law that had an enormous impact on the Korean population in California was the Webb-Heney Land Law. The law specified that only naturalized individuals, those that had become full U.S. citizens, were allowed to own land. Asians were considered aliens, or foreign citizens, and were ineligible for U.S. citizenship. Without naturalization, Koreans were prohibited from owning farms and homes. In addition, Koreans could not own boardinghouses, apartment buildings, or commercial buildings such as factories.

For Koreans who had invested their meager savings in such enterprises, the law had far-reaching and drastic consequences. Many Koreans who had already purchased property were forced to leave their investments. The law also gave the U.S. government the right to confiscate any land owned by aliens. Those with American-born children—who were considered citizens—often placed the property in their children's names to protect their assets. If property was discovered listed under the name of an American-born Korean child, however, it was subject to seizure. Many families accepted the risk despite the law.

The law essentially prevented Koreans from establishing their own businesses and drastically limited the amount of income immigrants could earn by forcing them into menial jobs. Without access to business and free enterprise, Koreans took undesirable jobs such as fruit pickers, miners, and janitors. The law was so effective in limiting the prospects of Koreans that eleven states—Arizona, Washington, Louisiana, New Mexico, Idaho, Montana, Oregon, Kansas, Utah, Wyoming, and Arkansas—enacted similar laws.

The Steward Incident

During the Yellow Peril, Korean Americans were at the mercy of the European American majority. Unarmed and outnumbered, Korean Americans had little protection when their lives were threatened. While others gave in to prejudice, Mary Steward, an orchard owner, refused to be bullied by her neighbors. When her workers were threatened, Mrs. Steward leaped to their defense.

Steward owned an orange grove in Upland, California. A devout Christian, Steward hired a number of Koreans to work as pickers. The Koreans established small settlements on Steward's property. Although neighbors complained, she refused to fire the Koreans.

Late one night, several neighbors approached the Korean camp, attacking the workers with sticks and rocks. Steward's neighbors said the Koreans would be killed if they did not leave immediately. According to Bong-Youn Choy in *Koreans in America*, Mrs. Steward said, "The minority Korean people in this great country of America have a right to live and work just as other nationalities. They are hard working, diligent and honest people who are struggling for a decent life."

Mrs. Steward reported the incident to authorities and received permission to obtain firearms for her workers in case of another attack. She instructed her workers to shoot anyone who threatened them. Then Steward contacted the newspapers, relating the incident in detail.

No further attacks were made on Mrs. Steward or her employees. In fact, after introducing her workers to the other growers, more Koreans found work in neighboring groves.

Interracial Marriages

While some Americans gave in to the Yellow Peril, others respected Koreans and even sought to marry these new immigrants. With few Korean women available for marriage, men looked for brides among other races. Marriages between Koreans, Chinese, and Japanese became more common, as did unions with Filipinos, Latinos, and Africans. These marriages found critics in both the Korean and Caucasian communities.

While the rate of interracial marriage was relatively small at the beginning of the twentieth century, men and women of European descent found happiness with Korean brides and grooms. The situation caused another furor among the anti-Korean supporters. For those already opposed to the Korean presence in America, the mixing of races represented a new type of peril. Those who believed Europeans to be a superior race protested the mixing of pure blood and what they considered to be the inferior blood of Koreans.

The United States government attempted to put an end to interracial marriage. In 1905, the California state government declared that any U.S. citizens who married immigrants would lose their citizenship and all rights reserved for citizens. The threats were enough to deter many marriages. Following California's lead, fifteen other states outlawed Korean-Caucasian marriages. Many of these laws were repealed in 1967 when the U.S. Supreme Court declared them unconstitutional.

White Americans were not the only ones to oppose mixed-race marriages. In Korea, marriage represented not only the union of a man and a woman, but also the joining of two families. Before a marriage was arranged, prospective mates were heavily researched, and good bloodlines were essential to making a match. Some in the Korean community considered interracial marriage as the dilution of pure Korean blood. One contemporary Korean American provided insight into the importance placed on pure Korean blood in Nazli Kibria's book, *Becoming Asian American:* "My parents don't emphasize marrying Korean—they demand, they threaten. The reasons they give are to keep Korean tradition alive, to keep the blood pure."[33]

Concerns were also raised about the family histories of these strange races. It was difficult for traditional Koreans to consider family status and honor when dealing with strange and unknown ethnic groups. Others viewed the marriages as an insult to their own race. They thought Koreans who selected mates from another ethnic background were turning their backs on their people. Syngman Rhee, a prominent Korean immigrant who later became the president of the Republic of South Korea, received widespread criticism from the Korean American community for marrying Francesca Donner, a Caucasian woman from Austria.

The Door Closes

The Yellow Peril climaxed in 1924 with the passage of the Oriental Exclusion Act. Persuaded by continuous public outcry that Koreans and Asians were a danger to white jobs and culture, Congress redesigned immigration laws. The Oriental

Exclusion Act denied Koreans entrance to the United States. The only exception granted was to students who wished to pursue an education at American universities. Estimates indicate that three hundred to six hundred Korean students entered the United States in the years following the act's passage.

The laws were a devastating blow to the Korean community. The Koreans already living in the United States were prevented from sending for their families. The wives, children, parents, and siblings of Korean Americans remained across the Pacific with no chance for reunion.

Those in the United States were not the only immigrants affected. Hundreds were already in the process of journeying to the United States, and those awaiting passage were instructed to return to their homes. These people, many of them families of Koreans already in America, had no homes to return to, having already sold their dwellings and possessions in preparation for the trip. Offered little or no compensation by the U.S. government, they returned to their villages and cities homeless and penniless.

In even worse positions were those already in Japan awaiting transport to America. Unable to continue their journey and with no money to pay for a return voyage, these Koreans were left stranded in a country whose domination they were trying to escape. Many were forced to re-

Syngman Rhee faced widespread criticism for marrying Francesca Donner, an Austrian woman.

main in Japan until they earned the money to return home.

Even picture brides were refused entry into America. With no wives for the single men, the Korean community could not increase, destroying the hopes of hundreds of Korean bachelors who longed for wives and families.

No Political Representation

The injustices plaguing the Korean American community were the result of fear

Ahn Chang-ho

One of the most well-respected Korean American social reformers, Ahn Chang-ho started his community service in 1899 at the age of twenty-two. After discovering that most Korean American housing areas were dirty and unpleasant, he worked to clean the neighborhoods house by house. He later tackled unemployment by creating labor-supply centers that contracted work for American businesses. Ahn enabled many Koreans in San Francisco to find employment and improve their living conditions.

He also founded the first Korean social group in San Francisco, the *Chin 'mok-hoe*, or Friendship Society, in 1903. He also played a role in the creation of the Mutual Assistance Society (*Kongnip Hyop Hoe*), the first Korean American political organization, two years later. Ahn returned to Korea in 1907 to assist with the independence movement but fled the country again after the Japanese takeover in 1910. Back in America, he organized the first Korean independence movement, as well as a Korean school.

Ahn believed that personal sacrifice was necessary to gain his homeland's freedom, and after years of sacrificing, Japanese police arrested Ahn in 1935 for participating in anti-Japanese activities. While in prison Ahn suffered a variety of illnesses due to the poor conditions. When he was finally released in 1938, he died only three days later.

Ahn Chang-ho dedicated his youth to improving living conditions for Korean Americans in San Francisco.

and racial prejudice among the European-descended majority. Many white Americans felt the only way to protect their jobs and livelihood was to stamp out what they perceived as the Asian threat. If conditions in the United States were inhospitable enough, they reasoned, the Koreans already in America might return to their homeland.

The key to oppression was to smother the Korean American voice. As long as they were denied citizenship, Koreans could not vote. Therefore, they could not prevent the passage of any discriminatory laws. As Koreans represented a small minority of the population, American lawmakers had little incentive to side with the immigrants or speak out against injustices. In fact, showing support for Koreans would make any politician unpopular among the white voting audience, and unpopular lawmakers rarely remain in office.

While Korean political organizations did exist, their focus was often homeland independence. Some groups did try to represent the Korean American population, but the Korean voice was largely ignored by Washington. Without a vote, Korean Americans had no power.

Naturalization Denied

During World War I, naturalization laws were changed once again. A special provision was created stating that *anyone* who served in the armed forces during the conflict would be granted citizenship. Korean Americans like Easurk Emsen Charr arrived at military headquarters eager to accept their new citizenship. For Charr and others like him, hope turned to bitter disappointment.

Asian ethnic groups, such as the Koreans, Chinese, and Japanese, were not listed among the eligible nationalities. The law had been created to allow easier citizenship for Europeans and other groups already allowed to become citizens. Although the provision used the word "anyone," it was really meant as a way for European immigrants to avoid long forms and naturalization tests.

In his autobiography, *The Golden Mountain*, Charr recalls challenging the provision's wording: "You mean ANYONE but ME,"[34] he complained. Charr had lived in the United States since he was ten years old, attended American schools and universities, and served in the army medical corps. He was fully assimilated, yet he was not allowed citizenship because of his race.

Charr was not alone in his disappointment. After living most of their lives in the United States, thousands of Korean immigrants desired the rights acquired with citizenship. They wanted to vote and own land, privileges denied them as resident aliens.

They embraced American culture, raised their children as Americans, and shed blood in American wars, yet they were still not accepted by mainstream America. The lack of support from state, local, and federal governments forced the Korean American community to look to one another for growth opportunities. Banding together, America's Koreans found the strength to move forward and find prosperity in the new land.

CHAPTER FOUR

Building Communities

Compared to other groups migrating to America at the same time, the number of Koreans was very small. Unlike the Japanese and Chinese, who might have ten thousand workers occupying a single plantation, the Koreans numbered only a few hundred per plantation. The geographic separation between plantations resulted in small pockets of Korean settlements rather than large communities.

Despite their small numbers and the distance between plantations, Korean laborers established a system of societies to allow communication between plantations. Religious, cultural, and social groups provided Koreans with forums for addressing the challenges of American life. As Korean Americans moved onto the mainland, these associations redefined themselves to meet the changing needs of their members.

These networks allowed Koreans to come together and share ideas, which further strengthened their sense of community. While some of these organizations were basic and useful only for the early years of immigration, others became complex political groups with thousands of members. Some of these organizations still exist today as testaments to the solidarity of the Korean American community.

Plantation Society

After their arrival, the first Korean Americans struggled against poverty and difficult working conditions. Many were lonely, frustrated, and discouraged, feeling life in the new country had been misrepresented to them. Some wished they had never come to America. As more Koreans came to America, however, the small population banded together, slowly creating an oasis of comfort and safety in Hawaii.

Korean immigrants established highly organized, self-governing social systems to maintain order in their new communities. Based on the systems used for centuries in Korea's rural communities, these village councils, known as *tong-hoe*, were created to promote law and order among the new immigrants. Within the *tong-hoe*, community affairs were decided by majority vote. Led by an elected leader, called the *tong-jang*, the councils established rules and dealt out punishment to those who violated the laws.

Additional offices were created for policemen and sergeants at arms to aid in the enforcement of the laws. One set of laws listed the following fines for those who broke the laws: "drunkenness, $1.00; drunken brawling, $5.00; gambling in Japanese or Chinese camps, $5.00."[35] If a person received three offenses, he was asked to leave the camp. The fines were used to finance Korean education and to care for the sick or elderly on the plantation.

The Korean National Association (pictured) worked to promote unity among Korean immigrants.

In 1907, as the number of Korean immigrants and councils grew, the *tong-hoe* were unified under a larger organization. The United Korean Society (*Hanin Hapsong Hyop-hoe*) was created to promote communication and solidarity among the individual plantation communities. Every Korean immigrant was expected to become a member. Dues were between three and five dollars per year, and the money was used to print newspapers and textbooks and provide welfare and education. Each year, representatives would meet to discuss concerns within the Korean American community, such as education and Korean freedom. The money raised by the organization was used to provide financial assistance to newcomers, support homeland independence, and promote Korean culture through the publishing of Korean-language books and newspapers.

The United Korean Society later joined with a similar organization, the California-based Mutual Assistance Society. Together, these two groups became the Korean National Association (KNA). The KNA became the voice of the Korean American people until World War II.

Church

Although village councils provided immigrants with law and order, other organizations were necessary to meet other social needs. Between 30 and 40 percent of Koreans entering the United States were already Christian, and many more were converted en route to Hawaii by shipboard missionaries. An estimated thirty Korean ministers were among the first immigrants to arrive in America. One of the first priorities of these immigrants was the creation of Christian churches.

The first congregation was established on the Hawaiian Island of Oahu on July 4, 1903, only six months after the arrival of the first immigrants. Although services were frequently held at the plantations, churches began to be constructed as more immigrants arrived. The Korean Evangelical Society was formed under the supervision of the Methodist Church in November 1903, almost a year after the arrival of the first immigrants. The society rented a house in Honolulu until it could afford to build a center. The society eventually became the Korean Methodist Church, the oldest Korean church in Hawaii.

In 1905, a second church, the Korean Episcopal Church, was created. The congregation moved to a number of sites before obtaining their own property in 1925. The facilities were constructed with money raised by the immigrants themselves. By 1918, almost forty different Christian congregations had formed.

On the mainland, Korean immigrants established churches immediately upon arrival. The first was the Korean Methodist Church in San Francisco. A congregation of fifty Koreans started meeting in 1905. They first utilized homes to conduct their services until a church building was acquired in 1911. Another Korean Methodist congregation formed in Los Angeles in 1904. Presbyterian churches were also among the earliest Korean American religious establishments, forming a congregation in Los Angeles in 1906.

Church was often the only opportunity for social interaction among the workers and their families. For instance, on the plantations the workers remained isolated from the outside world. Few had the opportunity to learn English or local customs. Many only knew their native language, so the church provided a venue for sharing news and experiences, quickly becoming the center of Korean society. Even those who were not Christian attended churches to meet other Koreans, and many converted to Christianity. The plantation owners approved of Korean churches. As Christians themselves, the owners believed the churches made the Korean workers more civilized and productive. One planter wrote, "These Koreans make the most sincere Christians I have ever known. They are becoming more and more the most desirable and efficient laborer."[36]

Attending church had many benefits beyond just socialization. An estimated 65 percent of Korean laborers were illiterate. Churches provided a means of education where adults could learn to read and write their own language. It is estimated that illiteracy among the Korean workers was wiped out within ten years of their arrival in Hawaii. Churches usually ran schools where Korean children were taught Korean language and customs. Churches sponsored performances of Korean music, dances, arts, and theater. When they went to church, many Koreans were reminded of home.

The church was also a symbol of hope. Many Koreans felt misled about the working conditions in America. Ministers provided words of comfort for work-weary laborers and uplifting sermons when they felt defeated.

Churches often helped those in need of food, clothing, and shelter. Most ministers were paid between $75 and $100 per month, and many church leaders gave the money back to the community, using it to feed and clothe needy parishioners. In one case, a minister named David Lee went without meals himself so he could feed members of the congregation. He later died of poor health, sacrificing himself for his people.

Ministers were not the only ones involved in helping the needy. Congregations often organized social programs, reaching out to members of the Korean community. Churchgoers provided emotional, and sometimes financial, support to those in need. Members made donations that were used to support the hungry or homeless.

The young men leading the churches were frequently scholars or political activists who had fled persecution in the homeland. The church was considered admirable employment for an educated man and drew notable ministers such as Syngman Rhee, the future president of the Republic of South Korea. With such leaders, the Korean churches became the heart of the Korean American political as well as religious scene. Immigrants gathered to discuss issues concerning both America and the homeland, giving voice to their fears and dreams.

Education

Religion went hand in hand with educational development. Education is an important part of the Korean tradition. In the

Syngman Rhee

Syngman Rhee was an important player in the Korean independence movement. Rhee's political career started at a young age. Born in 1874 or 1875 to an aristocratic *yangban* family, Rhee participated in an uprising against the Korean royal family in 1897. Rhee was sentenced to life in prison but was released after serving seven years of his sentence.

After his release, Rhee immigrated to Hawaii at the suggestion of his former prison mate Park Yong-man. Rhee received a master's degree in politics from Harvard and a PhD from Princeton. He became a teacher at, and later the principal of, the Korean Community School in Hawaii. In 1919, Rhee focused his efforts on homeland independence. He founded the Korean Christian Church and published two books and a newspaper, the *Pacific Weekly*. Through his active involvement, Rhee became regarded as the leader of the Korean American community.

While some members of the community considered Rhee a hero for his involvement with the independence movement, others questioned whether his motivation was to help the Korean American community or himself. When the provisional government was created in Shanghai, China, a committee named Rhee chief executive. He later named himself president, much to the dismay of others in his cabinet.

Rhee governed South Korea for twelve years, his presidency marred by corruption and intolerance. In 1960, Rhee was deposed when students marched to protest a fixed election. Rhee returned to Hawaii in exile, where he died in 1965.

Confucian hierarchy, scholars were at the top of the social pyramid, and becoming well educated was a noble and respected aspiration. Although only twenty-two children were recorded among the first immigrants, within six months there were about sixty Korean children in Hawaii. With the arrival of picture brides, the numbers of children continued to grow, and the Korean community began looking for means to educate its children.

American teachers arrived from the mainland. In public schools, Korean children learned to read and write English and were taught American history. In addition, Korean schools were established, either independently or as part of a church, to teach children Korean history and hangul, the Korean written alphabet.

The first Korean boarding school was established in 1906. Called the Korean Compound School, it was established by the Korean Methodist Church to educate Korean boys. A similar institution was created in 1914 to provide room and board to Korean girls who were attending public schools in Honolulu. Rather than travel from school to their homes, the children stayed at the school and were given lessons in Korean subjects. These two schools merged in 1918 to form the Korean Christian Institute. The institute's first principal was Syngman Rhee.

Plantation owners had mixed feelings regarding education. The owners viewed Korean children as the next generation of workers, a renewable resource to take their parents' place at death or retirement. While the owners approved of children learning English and basic math, other subjects made them uneasy. Planters were afraid that teaching Korean children about the Constitution and the Declaration of Independence would foster ideas of equality and independence. The owners did not mind literate workers, but they did not want their future labor source thinking they would achieve success anywhere other than on the plantation.

The plantation owners had reason for concern. In a survey conducted in 1922, only 0.5 percent of children said they desired to become laborers. Over 65 percent of the boys surveyed said they wished to become professionals or skilled workers. One planter observed, "They'll make intelligent citizens all right enough, but not plantation laborers—and that's what we want."[37]

Korean children on the mainland had educational challenges equal to their

Korean Alphabet

Consonants

ㄱ	ㄴ	ㄷ	ㄹ	ㅁ	ㅂ	ㅅ
g,k	n	d,t	r,l	m	p,b	s,sh

ㅇ	ㅈ	ㅊ	ㅋ	ㅌ	ㅍ	ㅎ
ng	j	ch	k	t	p	h

Vowels

ㅏ	ㅑ	ㅓ	ㅕ	ㅗ	ㅛ	ㅜ	ㅠ	ㅡ	ㅣ
a	ya	eo	yeo	o	yo	u	yu	eu	i

Hi. How are you?

안녕하세요

An nyeong ha se yo?

Fine. How are you?

네, 안녕하세요

Ne, an nyeong ha se yo?

In 1443, King Sejong the Great invented the Korean alphabet, known as hangul. The king believed the Chinese characters used by the scholars of the day did not represent the unique Korean national character and were too difficult for the common people to master. So he devised a Korean alphabet that even the uneducated could easily learn. Each hangul vowel and consonant is a diagram of the position of the mouth and tongue when the letter is spoken. Today, signs in hangul can be seen on stores in Koreatowns (urban areas where Koreans work and live) across the United States.

Hawaiian counterparts. Although mainland children had greater access to public schools, language barriers led to confusion and frustration. Most immigrant children could not speak English. When placed in classrooms, they did not understand the material, and did poorly in lessons. It takes between six and twelve months for someone to learn English, and without bilingual instructors, Korean children struggled in the classroom.

Further complicating matters, many teachers did not understand the difference between Koreans and other Asian groups, and were unable to recognize Korean children when they entered the classroom. Teachers often asked Chinese or Japanese students to translate for Korean children, unaware that the Korean language was vastly different from other Asian languages.

The Korean American community attempted to fill the void, creating schools like the Mugunghwa School in Los Angeles and the Korean-American Education Center in San Francisco. Established in the 1970s, both schools taught English and Korean language, as well as Korean studies on Sundays. These schools, and others like them, helped transition immigrant children into the American school system.

Korean immigrants viewed education as the only means to save their children from a life of harsh labor. Immigrant families supported education for their children. Parents saved money so their children could attend universities. To many, an American education was the key to a better life.

Kye

Korean Americans desired occupations beyond those of fruit pickers and plantation workers. Many were able to save money to start their own enterprises. Often these businesses were services for the Korean American community, such as barbershops and retail stores. Others opened larger businesses such as restaurants, hotels, and laundries. One family, the Rohs, operated three different businesses in Sacramento and Oakland, California, including a barbershop, a public bath, and a hotel, earning almost two thousand dollars a month from their combined enterprises.

Raising capital for these enterprises was not easy. Buildings and property cost tens of thousands of dollars. With monthly paychecks of less than twenty dollars, the money was more than most Koreans could earn in a lifetime. Unlike today, banks at the turn of the century could base loan refusals on race. Few financial institutions were willing to loan the immigrants money. On their own, Korean entrepreneurs did not have the financial means to start their own businesses.

To overcome this obstacle, the Korean society developed a unique lending system known as the *kye* (sometimes spelled *kea*). Immigrants interested in loans came together and formed lending groups. Members of the lending group each contributed a sum of money to a collective account. Each member would then take a turn withdrawing the money from the account to invest in a home or business. When able, the member would repay the money back to the *kye* with interest. When

Korean immigrant Yong Duckworth enrolled in the first grade at the age of thirty-five, determined to master the English language.

the loan was repaid, another member would take his or her turn to borrow the money.

In this way, many Korean Americans were able to find the funds necessary to start new businesses or purchase homes when financial institutions were unable or unwilling to provide resources. As Korean businesspeople became more affluent, they donated more money to the community, assisting additional neighbors. The success of early entrepreneurs helped the community flourish, allowing for the development of businesses that provided more goods and services. The *kye* system is still used in many Korean American communities today.

Communication

One of the most important businesses to arise out of the Korean community was the creation of Korean language newspapers. Newspapers were a clearinghouse of information for the Korean American community, providing information on events in the homeland. Written in the Korean language, the newspapers were also a means for Korean Americans to learn about American issues and culture.

The *Konglip Sinbo* was first printed in San Francisco in 1905. A newsletter of the Mutual Assistance Society, the paper described plantation conditions and brought news of the homeland. In 1909, *Shinhan Minbo*, America's first Korean newspaper, was published. The paper kept readers informed of events in the independence movement. Other newspapers soon followed, including the *Korean National Herald.*

Within the first decade of immigration, the Korean American community established five weekly magazines and four monthly newspapers. The industry further expanded with the production of books and other texts.

Ties That Bind

While churches and political organizations strengthened communal ties in America, most Korean Americans still maintained relationships with family in Korea. Sons and daughters in the United States supported their parents at home. Although wages were small, the laborers often managed to send money home. Some immigrants even saved enough to pay passage for their families to join them in America. Reunion with their families was a common goal among Korean Americans.

Another cause uniting the Korean American community was the struggle for homeland independence. For some Koreans, the move to America was intended to be temporary. They planned to return to Korea once the Japanese were ousted and political and economic conditions improved. Resistance groups were active in Korea, and those moving to America found ways to show their support for the movement. Workers saved money from their meager paychecks and sent the funds to the independence group.

Politics

Between 1903 and 1907, Korean Americans created more than twenty social, political, and cultural organizations. Most of the political groups focused on events in the homeland rather than those affecting Koreans in America. Ahn Jong-Su and Yun Pyong-Ku created the first Korean American political group in 1903. Called the New People's Society (*Sinmin-hoe*), members protested Japanese involvement in Korean affairs. Groups like the New People's Society held rallies to protest Japanese occupation of the homeland and also organized boycotts of Japanese goods.

These groups also acted on behalf of Korean Americans living in America and became the voice of the people. Many organizations sent delegates to world conferences, gaining support for the independence movement. The largest political group was the Korean National Association (KNA), which had its beginnings in the early plantation societies.

Because the Japanese government did not allow free speech in Korea, Koreans could not protest their treatment by the Japanese occupiers. Korean Americans became the voice of those still living in the homeland. The members of the KNA spoke against the injustices suffered by Korean citizens. After the 1904–1905 Russo-Japanese War, a war fought between Russia and Japan over who would control the Korean peninsula, members of the KNA petitioned to attend the peace talks in Portsmouth, New Hampshire. The group failed to gain recognition from world governments, leaving no one to

Military Might

While some Korean Americans sought to gain homeland independence through diplomacy, education, and peaceful demonstration, others decided that force was the only way to remove the Japanese from Korea. Korean American leaders created military academies in the United States to train men to fight the occupying Japanese forces.

The first training center was the Korean Youth Military Academy, created as part of the University of Nebraska in Hastings. Founded in 1909 by Park Yong-man, a patriot formerly imprisoned by the Japanese, the academy had twenty-seven students. The young men worked on farms during the day and practiced military exercises at night. Two years later, the first class of thirteen students graduated from the academy.

Encouraged by the success of Park's camp in Nebraska, other academies soon opened. Training facilities were established in California, Missouri, Wyoming, and the Hawaiian Islands. Another center was later established in Willows, California, to help train Korean American pilots.

Park continued to find support for his militaristic goals. In late 1910, the Korean National Association opened additional training centers in Hawaii and placed Park in charge of training. The facility grew to over fifty employees, including five instructors. In three years, over two hundred Korean Americans trained as part of Park's brigade.

Despite the success of the military centers in the United States, the centers were forced to close when the farms and plantations where the cadets worked did not renew their contracts. Without financial support, the centers could not remain open. Park's dream of a homeland invasion never materialized. In 1928, while establishing training centers in China, he was assassinated in Peking (now Beijing), China.

In hopes of freeing Korea from Japanese rule, Park Yong-man established military training centers for Korean American youth throughout the United States.

speak for the Korean people in the homeland. Many felt the lack of a Korean voice at the conference resulted in Japan gaining control over Korea.

After the conference, the KNA drafted a declaration to the Japanese government declaring they would never accept Japanese domination and would never stop fighting to free their homeland. On September 9, 1919, the KNA declared itself the only official voice of the Korean people, arguing that the Korean government was controlled by Japan and acted in the interests of the emperor instead of the Korean people. Copies of the declaration were sent to the ruling heads of nearly every world power. While many sympathized with the Korean American patriots, few wanted to risk Japan's displeasure, and nothing was done.

The Provisional Government

In 1919, Syngman Rhee approached the League of Nations as a representative of the KNA, requesting the establishment of a Korean government outside Korea. This provisional government would act in the interests of Koreans around the world until the homeland was freed from Japanese rule. The Japanese government refused to recognize the declaration, and Korea remained under Japanese control.

Later that same year, the KNA organized the Korean Liberty Congress in Philadelphia, Pennsylvania. The KNA invited the leaders of several North American organizations to the event, where they argued for their independence. The Korean Americans held parades and rallies,

Korean president Syngman Rhee favored a diplomatic solution to the Japanese occupation of Korea.

where the leaders of the KNA explained the plight of the Korean people under Japanese rule. The event culminated with Syngman Rhee reading the Proclamation of Independence of Korea, in which Koreans declared their freedom from Japan and declared the creation of a provisional government based in Shanghai.

By 1922, interest in the independence movement had waned. Fighting among their leaders divided the Korean American community. Leaders like Syngman Rhee desired diplomatic solutions to Japanese occupancy and were opposed to the militaristic ideas supported by Park Yongman, another political figure active in the independence movement. Korean Americans also began to take a greater interest in events directly related to themselves rather than to the homeland.

"I Am Korean"

Korean Americans were a people without a country. While under Japanese control, their homeland did not exist. In the United States they were not accepted and had no rights. By the 1940s, they were still without citizenship, and Japanese oppression continued at home. In 1941, events occurred that finally allowed Koreans to be recognized as a separate people from the Japanese.

At dawn on December 7, 1941, warplanes from the Empire of Japan attacked the United States naval fleet at Pearl Harbor in Hawaii. The surprise attack left almost twenty-four hundred Americans dead and another fourteen hundred wounded. Twenty-one ships and more than three hundred aircraft were either destroyed or damaged. The event shocked and outraged the American public and prompted U.S. entry into World War II.

For the Korean American community, the tragedy was also tinged with hope. It was the day they had long awaited. A Japanese defeat might finally mean freedom for the homeland, and Korean Americans rallied to support the war effort. Thousands of young Korean American men enlisted in the U.S. military, eager for an opportunity to fight against Korea's old enemy. For those too old to enlist, opportunities arose to act as fire wardens, national guards, and production workers in factories and shipyards.

Men were not the only volunteers. Korean American women assisted with the American Red Cross and the United Service Organization (USO). They helped organize cultural programs to educate Americans on Korean history and also supervised fund-raisers to support the war effort. Although their population numbered fewer than ten thousand, Korean Americans purchased almost a quarter of a million dollars in war bonds between 1942 and 1943, the largest amount purchased by a single group. More than twenty-six thousand dollars was sent to the president, and an additional four hundred dollars was given to the Red Cross.

Despite the show of support for America, the U.S. government still viewed Koreans as citizens of Japan, and Korean Americans met the same prejudice as the Japanese. Korean newspapers were monitored for signs of support for Japan, and Korean Americans were watched carefully to determine if they were spies. In 1942, President Franklin Roosevelt signed Executive Order 9066, which forced Japanese Americans out of their homes and businesses, and sent them to internment camps where they could be closely monitored for anti-American activities. Several government officials suggested that Korean Americans be sent to the internment camps along with the Japanese. In Hawaii, Koreans were asked to wear black badges on their clothing to identify them as Japanese citizens. Many refused to wear the emblems.

Members of the Korean American community approached the U.S. government and requested they be recognized as Koreans, not citizens of Japan. The government

The Tiger Brigade

The Korean American community's fierce patriotism did not end at the homeland. After the attack on Pearl Harbor, Korean American men flooded military recruitment centers to offer their lives for freedom. While many Korean Americans worked behind the scenes as spies or translators, others were assigned to mixed Asian units. In California, however, an all-Korean unit was created.

Called the Tiger Brigade, the unit was part of the California National Guard. Established on December 29, 1941, 50 Koreans signed up for service. The number later swelled to 109, one-fifth of the total Korean population in Los Angeles. Participants' ages ranged from eighteen to sixty-five, and each man or woman received military training for four hours a day each weekend. Members marched in parades as Korean girls waved Korean flags. Bands from the U.S. Army joined the brigade in both the American and Korean anthems.

Although the Tiger Brigade never saw battle, the unit gained visibility and support for the Korean American community.

agreed, and organizations like the United Korean Committee, a group organized in 1941 to help unify Korean Americans in support of the Allied forces during World War II, distributed identification badges labeled "I am Korean" and stickers bearing an image of the Korean flag to help differentiate between Japanese and Koreans.

Despite the public mistrust of Koreans, the U.S. government employed more than 250 Korean Americans during the war. Korean students with knowledge of the Japanese language earned posts within the U.S. government working as interpreters. The Koreans were responsible for decoding and translating Japanese documents, and some even went to Korea and Japan to work as agents. During the Japanese relocation, the government relied on Korean interpreters to communicate with members of the Japanese community who did not speak English.

Fifty years after their arrival, Korean Americans finally gained some measure of acceptance by the American government. Their involvement in World War II helped soften prejudices and elevated them from enemy aliens to invaluable contributors to the war effort. While they still encountered discrimination, the years following the war presented Korean Americans with more prominent, high-profile careers and opened the door to greater opportunities.

CHAPTER FIVE

The Second Wave

E ven after World War II, many Americans had never heard of Korea. Statements of "I am Korean" brought confused stares from Euro-Americans who thought Korea was a province in China or an island near Japan. Events following the war, however, soon catapulted Korea to the forefront of the American consciousness.

Only a few years after World War II, another war sent members of the American armed forces to a strange country, and the formerly invisible kingdom was soon known by many Americans. The Korean War changed the face of the Korean American population. As Koreans once again faced poverty and devastation, the U.S. government relaxed immigration laws allowing Koreans entry. As Koreans came to the United States, a new generation of immigrants struggled to find their place in America.

The Korean War

After the defeat of Japan in World War II, Allied leaders decided to grant Japanese territories independence. One provision of the agreement indicated that colonies like Korea would first go through a Western educational process overseen by the Allied countries. The Soviet Union had

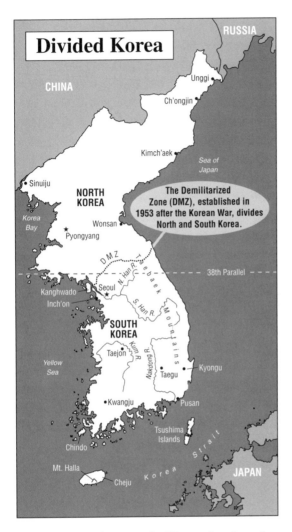

Divided Korea

RUSSIA

CHINA

Unggi

Ch'ongjin

Sinuiju

Kimch'aek

Sea of Japan

NORTH KOREA

Korea Bay

Wonsan

★ Pyongyang

The Demilitarized Zone (DMZ), established in 1953 after the Korean War, divides North and South Korea.

DMZ

N. Han R.

T e b a e k

38th Parallel

Kanghwado

Seoul

Inch'on

S. Han R.

SOUTH KOREA

M o u n t a i n s

Taejon

Kum R.

Yellow Sea

Nakdong R.

Taegu

Kyongu

Kwangju

Pusan

Tsushima Islands

Chindo

K o r e a

S t r a i t

Mt. Halla

Cheju

JAPAN

northern half and America the southern half. The Soviets agreed.

In the years after World War II, the American government showed no indication of uniting Korea as promised. Tensions began to build between Communist North Korea and its southern neighbor as the North Korean government, led by Kim Il-sung, attempted to unify the country by force. In the early hours of June 25, 1950, North Korean troops invaded South Korea, prompting a coalition of twelve nations, including the United States, to send troops to oust the invaders. Although the conflict lasted only three years, the United States Department of Defense reported that almost fifty-five thousand American soldiers and an estimated 4 million Koreans—approximately two-thirds of them civilians—had lost their lives.

The Korean War had a lasting effect on the Korean people, and particularly on their immigration patterns to America. In the aftermath of the war, millions of Koreans became refugees, their homes and land destroyed by shelling. The Korean economy was devastated, and the threat of starvation loomed for many families. Eui-Young Yu, a schoolboy during the war, described the scene on his family's return to Seoul:

When we returned home to Seoul, we learned that my uncle (my mother's brother) had been killed by the communists. He was considered an enemy of the people because he owned a hardware store and was rich by their standards. We also saw half our house destroyed by an American

expressed an interest in Korea for decades and agreed to this plan. Soviet soldiers moved into Manchuria, a province in China situated just north of Korea. Although they were allies, many Western governments did not approve of Soviet communism and feared an increase in Soviet power if it controlled the entire Korean Peninsula. Before Soviet troops could move into Korea, Allied leaders suggested temporarily splitting Korea into two halves along the thirty-eighth parallel, allowing the Soviets control of the bomb. The house was bombed during a battle between UN and North Korean forces. Half of our church was also destroyed.[38]

For families like Yu's, the options were few. Like their countrymen and women a half century earlier, the Korean people again faced poverty, starvation, and uncertainty. Many Koreans decided to leave their homeland in search of a better life. With American immigration laws once again favoring Asians, many Koreans migrated to the United States.

The Door Reopens

Near the conclusion of the Korean War, the United States relaxed immigration laws banning Asians from entering the country. In 1952, Congress passed the McCarran-Walter Immigration and Naturalization Act. Designed to keep track of immigrants in an era of anti-Communist sentiment, this law established a quota system based on country of origin. Three percent of the existing immigrant population was allowed to enter. At the time, the Korean population in the United States was estimated at ten thousand. The act allowed only a trickle of new immigrants, approximately three hundred per year.

Although it did not greatly increase Korean immigration, the McCarran-Walter Act had an important provision. It finally allowed Koreans and other Asians to become naturalized American citizens. They gained the freedoms previously denied them during the Yellow Peril era. As naturalized citizens, Korean Americans could now own land and vote. After years of enduring prejudice and humiliation without representation, Korean Americans could have a voice in politics. In the following

Displaced by the devastation of the Korean War, many Koreans like these fled with their belongings and immigrated to the United States.

years, hundreds of Korean Americans applied for and gained citizenship.

Immigration laws changed again in 1965. The quota system was abolished, allowing even more Koreans to enter the United States. The Immigration Act of 1965 gave preference to spouses, children, and parents of American citizens. Family reunions were once again made possible as many Korean Americans brought their families to the United States. Preferences were also given to immigrants with professional backgrounds and educations. An estimated three hundred thousand Koreans flocked to the United States between 1965 and 1980. Twenty years after the passage of the act, the Korean population had risen from 1 percent of the Asian American population to 11 percent.

Immigrants in this second wave were even more diverse than their predecessors, the predominantly male laborers who moved to the plantations at the dawn of the century. The second wave brought different demographics into the country, including more women and members of Korea's middle and upper classes. From single young women to war orphans to well-educated families, the new wave continued to shape the face of the Korean American community.

War Brides

The first noticeable change in America's Korean population was the sudden rise in female immigrants. At the end of World War II and of the Korean War, American soldiers (GIs) desired to return home with Korean brides. The American government recognized that changes needed to be made to immigration laws to accommodate the war veterans. The War Brides Act allowed the wives and children of U.S. soldiers to come to America regardless of the quota. In the 1950s and 1960s, between 70 and 80 percent of all Korean immigrants were females—most of them war brides. Estimates are that twenty-eight thousand women came to the United States as spouses of U.S. servicemen.

For a war bride, the journey to America was filled with both fear and excitement. Unlike many immigrants who were coming to join their families, the war brides were leaving their families behind in Korea. These women left their homes for a completely alien country with a new language and customs. Many parents did not approve of their daughters moving so far from home. Kyong-ae Price recalled her father's reaction to her decision to move to America in *East to America*: "A week before we left Korea, I told my father that I had married an American and we were going to America. He was shocked, but he could not do anything. Anyway, he wasn't responsible for my life. He told me that he would consider me dead and not think of me as his daughter."[39]

American families were also cautious about the war brides. Families still clinging to racial bias considered Korean brides exotic and worried about cultural differences. While some brides were accepted into their husbands' families, others met with derision. War brides were often lonely, even among other Koreans. Rather than receiving increased status by marrying an American, many of the war brides encountered discrimination by other members of the Korean community. War brides were regarded as poor and ignorant, women who had married their husbands to escape poverty. Others were accused of being prostitutes. Women who married Americans were referred to as "dirty women" and were called names like *yangkongju*, or Western princesses.

Many war brides were Christian and through their religion learned about gender equality. Moving to America meant escape from the strict Confucian hierarchy. In America, they could follow their dreams and were not restricted to staying at home. However, life in America was not always what they expected. Although some brides came to the United States to pursue personal goals, others dreamed of being taken care of in luxury. In Korea, women traditionally cared for the home and did not have careers of their own. Some thought it would be the same in America. However, they soon learned that two paychecks were necessary for family survival. Many were not prepared to work and encountered difficulties finding jobs due to lack of experience and language barriers.

In other cases, husbands expected their wives to be the stereotypical subservient

Pictured with her American husband and their child, Yoong Soon was the first of thousands of Korean war brides in the United States.

women that Korean culture dictated. Some men thought their wives would wait on them like servants. They were unprepared when their wives desired freedom and independence. A high rate of divorce developed among GIs and war brides due to cultural differences, language barriers, and unequal expectations.

Adoptees

Another side effect of the war was a large number of orphaned and displaced children. Thousands of Korean children were left homeless, many emotionally scarred after witnessing their parents killed in the war. As families grappled with starvation, parents and surviving family sent children to orphanages, hoping their offspring would have a better chance of survival.

In addition to the war orphans, thousands of Korean women are believed to have borne out-of-wedlock children to American servicemen. In Korea, having a child out of marriage brings shame not only to the woman but also to her entire family. Rather than bear the stigma of being an unwed mother, many women sent their children to orphanages. Bloodlines are very important in Korea, and half-American children had no place in Korean society. Some women faced brutal punishment for their pregnancies. Rather than face death for their children or them-

selves, mothers gave up their children to spare them lives of degradation.

Adoption is not widely practiced in Korea. The emphasis placed on continuing the family lines prevents many couples from adopting orphans. For those who do choose adoption, the process is often done in secret so no one will know the child is not a biological son or daughter. Although the Korean government now offers incentives to adoptive families, no provisions existed immediately after the wars.

The combination of social tradition and economic hardship left a bleak future for the children in Korea's orphanages. In the latter part of the 1950s, the future of Korea's orphans brightened. In 1955, an American named Henry Holt and his wife Bertha petitioned Congress to adopt eight

War Brides

The number of Korean women entering the United States skyrocketed as American servicemen brought brides home from Asia. Often these women were the focus of prejudice from both Korean and American families. In Elaine H. Kim and Eui-Young Yu's book, *East to America: Korean American Life Stories*, Kyong-ae Price recalls her mother-in-law's reaction to learning her son had a Korean wife: "She replied that he should not marry a foreigner, especially a Korean girl. Korea was so tiny and different, she said; a Korean girl could not survive in a big country like the United States."

Brides could not even find solace among the Korean American community.

Many Koreans considered war brides to be little better than prostitutes. Instead of finding comfort, women found derision. One war bride recalls in Nancy Abelmann and John Lie's book *Blue Dreams*: "Of course, I love to see our people and eat our own food that I crave and talk about our past in Korea. . . . But I don't want to see them, because I don't want to be looked down on by them. I've suffered and waited for the day when people would say I am a wonderful housewife. But it never came to me."

While many of these marriages survived the stress of prejudice, others did not. A large number of marriages between war brides and soldiers ended in divorce.

Thousands of Korean children like this boy have been adopted into American families since the end of the Korean War.

Korean children. A year later, the Holts founded Holt International Children's Services, an organization dedicated to intercountry adoptions. It is estimated that over one hundred thousand Korean children have been adopted by American families since the 1950s, with over sixty thousand adopted between 1980 and 1998 alone.

In 1982, a second option arose for half-American children still living in Korea. The American government recognized the difficult conditions facing abandoned children of U.S. servicemen. As offspring of American citizens, these children possessed claims to citizenship themselves. The American government thus passed the Amerasian Immigration Act of 1982. This law allowed children fathered by U.S. citizens between 1950 and 1982 to immigrate to the United States with full citizenship.

Half-American children were now eligible to enter the United States and seek opportunities not afforded to them in Korea.

Professionals

While war brides and children added significantly to the Korean American population, well-educated professionals have been the majority of second-wave immigrants. From 1965 until the present, 70 percent of new immigrants arriving in America possessed college educations, unlike the poor and uneducated members of the first wave. Many held respected positions such as doctors, nurses, and pharmacists in Korea. Faced with workplace saturation and stiff competition at home, these white-collar workers looked abroad for job opportunities.

Honhyol—Less than Human

In Korea, few actions bring a woman greater shame than bearing a child out of wedlock. Even worse is having a mixed race child. Elizabeth Kim was the result of her mother's relationship with a U.S. serviceman after the Korean War. As a child in Korea, Kim remembered being spat on and called *honhyol*, an insult meaning "despised" or "less than human."

According to Kim's controversial account, as a toddler she watched her uncle and grandfather hang her mother. The family desired to rid themselves of the shame of a mixed-race child and wanted to send the child to live with another family as a servant. Kim's mother refused, hiding her daughter in a basket when family members came to take the child. After her mother's death, the relatives discovered Kim's hiding place and took her to an orphanage.

In her autobiography, *Ten Thousand Sorrows*, Kim describes the traditions that did not accept her mixed birth: "In Asian culture, in which bloodline and honor are immensely important, there has historically been an intolerance for mixed race children. National pride is deeply ingrained, and in Korea the intense love for the country's heritage and traditions has its darker side of hatred for anything that taints the purity of that heritage."

In addition to greater education, the second-wave professionals also possessed more money than the previous wave. While the first group could barely afford passage, Korean professionals arrived with capital to help support them as they started their new lives. It is estimated that the average immigrant has brought between twenty-five thousand and fifty thousand dollars from Korea, using the money to set up businesses or sustain the family until a home or job is acquired.

New Opportunities

In the early twentieth century, Korean immigrants could expect to find only low-paid menial jobs such as cleaning or field labor. Today a world of opportunities exists. Korean Americans are finding jobs as professors, scientists, and engineers.

A large percentage of Korean Americans have started small businesses. Korean Americans have the highest self-employment rate of any other ethnic group. An estimated 28 percent of Korean American men and 20 percent of Korean American women have started their own businesses. Among these are restaurants, clothing stores, nail salons, and other service establishments.

Perhaps the largest percentage of Korean businesses are grocery stores. In a survey conducted in 1983, Korean Americans reported owning eight hundred of the twelve hundred greengrocers (fruit and vegetable markets) in New York. The relatively low operating costs of these ventures allow Korean Americans to purchase the stores when the previous owners retired.

The apparent success of Korean American business comes at a high price, however. An estimated 90 percent of those operating grocery stores and other shops are college-educated professionals. A large percentage have degrees in education, finance, and even medicine. However, language barriers and workplace discrimination prevent these individuals from finding employment in their fields. In Nancy Abelmann and John Lie's book, *Blue Dreams*, one immigrant described his frustration with the language barrier: "People look at me like I am a savage because I don't speak English right."[40]

Many physicians do not know English well enough to pass mandatory certification exams. In one study, an estimated thirteen thousand medical professionals worked as orderlies or nurses because they were unable to pass the English language test. Even those that do pass the exams are often put aside in favor of Caucasian doctors. In Nazli Kibria's book *Becoming Asian American*, the daughter of a Korean American doctor described what occurred when a white doctor moved to their small community: "Even though my father had done all this great service for so long, there were people who just abandoned him."[41]

Underemployment often leads to frustration. One survey suggested that as many as 78 percent of America's Korean American greengrocers had college degrees. Dong Hwan Ku is one of the many professionals not working at a level commensurate with his education. A shop owner, he says,

In my own case, I am a cripple without any American education. There's no

These Korean American women in Virginia run their own beauty salon. Many Korean Americans operate successful small businesses.

way out. I just have to continue to work hard. I have a college degree in architecture from Hong Ik University in Seoul, but look at me now. I am sick and tired. I feel defeated. The prospects for my further growth are limited. What kind of future is there? American-born Koreans, when they grow up, will face race discrimination, even if they are born here. It's not fair.[42]

Shop owners and their families work long hours, often depending on family members to provide free labor in order to survive. Describing his average day, Dong Hwan Ku states: "I work in this shop fourteen hours a day, seven days a week. My wife works here nine hours a day. The only other thing we do is go to church. But even then, we can't even go together; one person has to mind the store."[43]

For weary Korean Americans, returning to the homeland is not an option. After sinking all their savings into businesses, they find it impossible to return. One Korean American shopkeeper lamented: "Even if you come here with lots of money, it all gets tied up in payments— house, car, and so on—it's different from Korea, you can't leave."[44]

Model Minority

Despite the disparity between education levels and employment, a number of government offices choose to use the high rate of self-employment among Korean Americans as an example of new immigrants achieving the American dream. One of the most hard-fought labels in the Korean American community has been that of the "model minority." The model minority idea claims that Korean Americans arrive in America with very little and rise above adversity through hard work.

While it is true many Korean Americans have found wealth and success, advocates of the model minority theory do not take into account the background of Korean entrepreneurs. They look solely at the number of self-employed Koreans. To a person with a background in medicine, running a grocery store is hardly considered a sign of success.

The model minority is frustrating to Koreans and other ethnic minorities. Opponents argue that the idea promotes stereotypes. Many feel the model minority idea implies that other ethnic groups are lazy and unmotivated, and that these others should follow the example set by Korean Americans. Advocates are not considering the differences in class and education between Korean Americans and other immigrants. The model minority stereotype has led to tensions and hostility between Koreans and other ethnic groups. For example, as Korean Americans succeeded in depressed urban areas, conflicts erupted.

Success in South Central

In the last several decades when shop owners in low-income areas retired, Korean Americans stepped in to fill the void. Often the urban neighborhoods were economically depressed. One such area was South Central Los Angeles. A predominantly Hispanic and African American neighborhood, the region had a reputation for poverty and was the scene of the 1965 Watts race riots. Urban impressionist K.W. Lee commented on the influx of Korean Americans into these economically depressed areas stating, "With their eyes wide open, Koreans walked into violent inner city areas. They just dived with reckless abandon into the places where the most deprived people live, without thinking of the dynamics of the neighborhood."[45]

While many neighbors accepted the influx of Korean Americans into the area, others did not. Cultural differences often led to misunderstandings. For example, in Korea it is considered disrespectful to look someone in the eye. In America, many saw the lack of eye contact by Koreans as a sign of disregard. Limited knowledge of English also led to misunderstandings between customers and shopkeepers.

When Korean businessmen started to earn profits from their shops, they were criticized for purchasing luxury cars and parking them in front of their stores. Neighbors saw this as the Koreans flaunting their wealth and developed resentment toward them, feeling the shop owners attained wealth acquired through their pocketbooks. Korean store owners were frequently beaten and robbed, but with all their finances invested in their businesses, they remained in urban areas. In the early 1990s, racial tensions in Los Angeles erupted with devastating ferocity.

Sa-i-gu: The Los Angeles Riots

On April 29, 1992, a jury acquitted four Los Angeles police officers—Theodore

Some people resent the success of Korean American shop owners like this herbalist sweeping in front of his Los Angeles store.

Briseno, Stacey Koon, Laurence Powell, and Timothy Wind—of felony assault charges in the beating of Rodney King, an African American whom they had stopped for speeding. With the officers' actions caught on tape, Americans everywhere were shocked by the verdict, and the wave of outrage was felt strongest in South

Central Los Angeles. Thousands of Latinos and African Americans descended on the neighborhood, looting businesses, overturning cars, and setting fires. Many Korean businesses were specifically targeted by rioters. Called *sa-i-gu* (4-2-9) by the Korean American community, in reference to the date, the riots were unlike those ever seen in America. In his book, *A Different Mirror*, author Ronald Takaki likened the scene to the Middle East: "The rioting and the murderous melee on the streets resembled the fighting in Beirut and the West Bank. The thousands of fires burning out of control and the dark smoke filling the skies brought back images of the burning oil fields of Kuwait during Desert Storm."[46]

Mingled with these scenes of destruction were images of Korean American shopkeepers, standing on rooftops and brandishing weapons to protect their businesses. The media grabbed on to this militant image, portraying the Korean Americans as gun-toting vigilantes. One Korean American woman argued against the negative portrayal: "They depict us like crazy people holding guns, but they have no idea of how many Koreans died doing business."[47]

One important event leading to the attacks on Korean American businesses was the murder of Latasha Harlins by shopkeeper Soon Ja Du prior to the King case. In March 1991, the fifteen-year-old Harlins reportedly refused to pay $1.79 for a bottle of orange juice. In the ensuing argument, Du shot and killed Harlins. Surveillance tape footage of the incident was shown across Los Angeles's news stations, angering African Americans. Al-

Armed with rifles, two Korean grocers in Los Angeles protect their store from looters after the 1992 Rodney King verdict.

though Du was found guilty of voluntary manslaughter, she did not receive any jail time. Instead, Du was placed on five years' probation. The ruling increased racial tensions, as many people felt the girl's death warranted a stiffer sentence.

The Aftermath

The King verdict was the match that lit the racial powder keg. The riots left fifty-eight people dead and twenty-four hundred injured. More than eleven thousand people were arrested. The aftermath was particularly devastating to Korean Americans. Of the reported $717 million in damages, an estimated $350 million was to Korean businesses alone. More than fifteen hundred Korean businesses were destroyed.

Dong Hwan Ku was a witness to the riots. In *East to America*, he describes a group of rioters entering his store:

After the Rodney King verdict, the other stores around here were broken into. The windows were smashed. One market down the street was completely looted of everything of value. People broke down my door and started looting until I showed them I had a gun. At first, they said, "Go ahead and shoot." And kept putting things into their pockets. So I shot one round into the air. They threw down what they had and left. The police didn't even get here until much later.[48]

For many immigrants, these businesses represented their life's work. After enduring long hours with little pay, they were not willing to let their businesses go up in smoke without making an effort to save them. Although they asked for police assistance, law enforcement response was often delayed. Departments did not want to send in officers until the riots cooled, but by then it was too late for most stores. Some shop owners indicated that police did arrive but did not do anything while the stores were being looted. One Korean American student observed: "The police weren't there for us, it blew my mind."[49] Shopkeepers armed themselves to protect their goods.

The government did offer some relief after the riots, and shop owners tried to collect on insurance policies. However, language continued to be a barrier; those who did not understand the government forms did not receive the promised financial aid. Without capital, stores and businesses could not be rebuilt. In the end, many Korean Americans never recovered from the riots and lost everything they owned.

In a country that has long prided itself on its melting pot image, the riots were disturbing evidence that racial inequality was not an issue buried in the distant past. Many historians liken the Los Angeles riots to the civil rights movement. The riots are considered the Korean American community's trial by fire, the day they finally came to the forefront of the American consciousness.

No longer invisible Americans, the riots left Korean Americans contending with another stereotype. Caught between stereotypes of model citizens and gun-toting zealots, the Korean American community still struggles to find its identity.

CHAPTER SIX

Becoming Korean American

As Koreans continue to enter the United States, they look to find their place in society. Korean Americans struggle to define their identities as both Koreans and Americans. They must balance the ancient traditions of the homeland with the sometimes conflicting ideas of mainstream America. While some Korean Americans live and work among their compatriots, finding comfort in reminders of home, others may be the only Korean for miles.

Adults are not the only Koreans questioning their identities. Young Korean Americans also strive to find their place. Generational gaps can sometimes cause friction in families as American-born children rebel against their parents' values. Adoptees who have never seen Korea or had exposure to any of its customs are left in cultural limbo. They are not fully American or Korean, and some are not accepted into either culture.

The Korean American community is working to help its members find balance. A wide range of programs has been developed to educate Korean Americans on the homeland's past and help foster national pride and understanding. These programs also allow non-Korean Americans to understand Korea's unique culture. More young people are discovering what it means to be Korean in America.

Koreatowns

The migration of Koreans to America led to the development of concentrated Korean enclaves in urban areas. These small cities-within-cities have come to be known as Koreatowns. Koreatowns represent cultural hubs, areas where new immigrants can network with others sharing their common experiences.

In Koreatowns, new immigrants find a slice of home. Korean Americans can find comfort in native foods, and signs beckon to shoppers in hangul. Those that have not yet learned English can find Korean-language grocery stores, barbershops, and other businesses.

The first Koreatown developed in Reedley, California, as a neighborhood for Koreans employed as fruit pickers. Today, the largest of the Koreatowns covers a five-hundred-block area in Los Angeles, stretching from Santa Monica Boulevard to Pico. This Koreatown is ten times larger than both Chinatown and Japantown combined, and is home to almost fifty thousand Korean Americans. Data from the 2000 census indicates that almost one-quarter of America's Korean population lives within five counties in California. Another large Koreatown is found in New York. Situated on Thirty-second between Broadway and Fifth Avenue, the New York Koreatown and the surrounding area are home to almost two hundred thousand Korean Americans, about 16 percent of the nation's Korean population. Other significant Korean neighborhoods exist in Chicago, Honolulu, and Houston.

Critics of Koreatowns argue that by isolating themselves within an all-Korean community, Korean Americans prevent assimilation and do not gain the full American experience. Korean Americans can live their entire lives in Koreatowns and never need to learn English. To others, Koreatowns are an oasis of familiarity in a

A strip-mall sign in Koreatown in Los Angeles advertises a variety of services available to the local Korean American community.

strange land. New immigrants can gradually learn American language and customs through personal interactions, language classes, and the media without being completely thrust into an unknown environment.

Il-se: **The First Generation**

Many of those living in Koreatowns are the *il-se*, or first-generation Korean immigrants. The *il-se* are those who arrived in the United States as adults. The *il-se* are not only the plantation laborers who arrived at the beginning of the twentieth century but also the well-educated men and women that continue to enter the United States today.

In general, their assimilation is the most difficult. When they arrive in America, the *il-se* are faced with alien customs and language. Fitting in can be a daunting task. Many speak little or no English, and language barriers may make finding employment difficult. Like the first generation of previous decades, the *il-se* are often forced to take low-wage jobs. They experience frustration working beneath their education levels. The *il-se* focus on education for their children so the next generation will not be forced to do menial jobs.

The *il-se* usually possess the strongest ties to the homeland, having been raised there most of their lives. To the *il-se*, the issue of a united Korea, the reunification

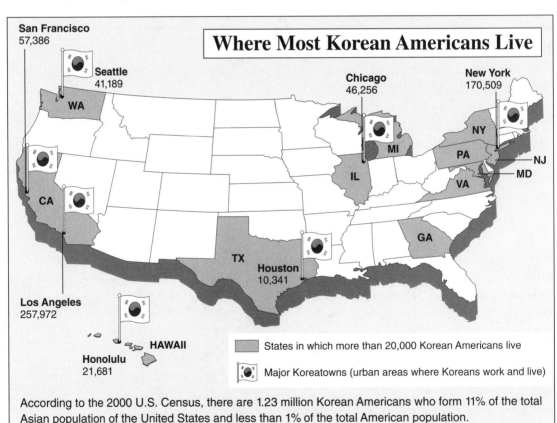

Where Most Korean Americans Live

San Francisco
57,386

Seattle
41,189

WA

Chicago
46,256

New York
170,509

NY

MI

PA

NJ

MD

IL

VA

CA

GA

TX

Houston
10,341

Los Angeles
257,972

HAWAII

Honolulu
21,681

States in which more than 20,000 Korean Americans live

Major Koreatowns (urban areas where Koreans work and live)

According to the 2000 U.S. Census, there are 1.23 million Korean Americans who form 11% of the total Asian population of the United States and less than 1% of the total American population.

of North and South Korea, is an important topic, much as homeland freedom was a century earlier. They desire to see both North and South Korea become a unified country, much as earlier Korean Americans wished to end Japanese occupation. Many still have family—siblings or parents—in Korea, and they take an active interest in homeland politics and events.

Of all the Korean Americans, the *il-se* are the most likely to adhere to native customs and traditions. Some may wear native clothing, particularly during special occasions such as weddings. Korean foods, such as kimchi, spicy pickled cabbage, are still a staple in households. Many *il-se* still practice Confucianism and hold family relationships to the guidelines prescribed in the hierarchy, expecting obedience from children and subservience from wives. Members of this group often experience confusion or frustration when other members of the community or family fail to adhere to the social hierarchy. In *Making More Waves*, Lisa Park notes her mother's resistance to Lisa's attempts at assimilation: "You not American. Why you try to be American?"[50]

Il-chom-o-se

Il-chom-o-se, or 1.5 (one-and-a-half) generation, is the term Korean Americans use to describe those born in Korea but who arrived in the United States as children or young adults. Members of this group bridge the divide between the new and old countries, embracing aspects of both cultures. Unlike their parents, many of these individuals have attended American

schools and gained knowledge of English. The *il-chom-o-se* are usually fluent in both Korean and English, and often act as translators for their parents.

The *il-chom-o-se* possess a unique blend of both Korean and American customs. Many members of this group still remember Korea and have ties to the homeland, although the connections are not usually as strong as those of the *il-se*. The need for homeland reunification is not always felt as strongly by the *il-chom-o-se* as it is by their parents. One Korean American student described the older generation in *Blue Dreams:* "Their idea of Korean identity is entirely from the 1960s, unchanged."[51]

For the *il-chom-o-se*, the need to balance tradition and the new American culture is challenging. Some are embarrassed by the older generations of parents and grandparents and their elders' need to cling to old ideas and customs. One 1.5 generation immigrant describes his feelings in *Becoming Asian American:* "I felt uncomfortable when I was in a crowd of Korean people, not when I was with Americans."[52] Disputes arise between the generations as the *il-chom-o-se* adopt American ideas of independence instead of traditional customs of subservience.

The *il-chom-o-se* are frequently exposed to discrimination in schools, particularly upon first arriving, when they have not yet learned the English language. These children are often scorned by their peers for eating Korean foods. To prevent teasing, *il-chom-o-se* sometimes try to distance themselves from their Korean heritage. Faced with teachers that

As Korean Americans become more Americanized, traditions such as bowing to one's parents during a wedding ceremony may become obsolete.

cannot pronounce their Korean names, many adopt Americanized names to better fit in with their peers. *Il-chom-o-se* youths also might rebel against the ideas of their parents by wearing American clothing and dating outside their own ethnic group.

In the book *East to America: Korean American Life Stories*, Dredge Kang describes his conservative parents' negative reactions to his American dress and attitudes:

> I still try to please my parents, but I also have to please myself. My father tells me that I will go to hell for having multiple piercings. It seems that I have destroyed the pressure points, unbalanced my *ki* [life force], and let all the *bok* [good fortune, happiness] flow out of me. My mother says that my bald head, multiple piercings, goatee, and expensive clothing make me look like a peasant in a potato sack . . . shaming the whole family.[53]

I-se: The Second Generation

The second generation, or *i-se*, are the offspring of the *il-se* or *il-chom-o-se*. These American-born children are almost fully assimilated into the American culture. While their experiences are similar to the *il-chom-o-se*, the *i-se* face unique challenges. First, having been raised only in America, the *i-se* speak little or no Korean. The language barrier results in miscommunication between children and their parents and other elders. Many encounter derision from other Koreans for their lack of knowledge of traditions and language. *I-se* children are teased by other Koreans for not being fully Korean, yet they are not treated as Americans either.

Because of their physical differences from Caucasian peers, Korean American children are not always readily accepted into the American culture, although this is the group with which they identify themselves. Even though they speak perfect English, *i-se* are often bombarded by questions about where they were born and their ethnic background. When they identify themselves as American, *i-se* are often met with disbelief.

Wearing American-style fashions and possessing a preference for American foods, the *i-se* develop American attitudes and behaviors, which sometimes put them at odds with their parents. While their parents consider scholarly pursuits the highest priority, their *i-se* children sometimes prefer to engage in other activities, like going to the mall or playing video games like other American children. The situation is particularly frustrating for underemployed parents who feel education is the only means for their children to enter prestigious universities and occupations. The children, however, oftentimes would rather socialize with friends than focus solely on school.

Author Elaine Kim was born in the United States. Growing up in an area where there were few Koreans, she describes her efforts to find acceptance:

I drank a lot to be cool. I had convinced myself that I was "American," whatever that meant, all the

A Gangster's Life

Like their parents, Korean immigrant children struggle to adapt to life in a new country. Thrust into schools, these children may be ridiculed for their appearance or ethnic background. A limited knowledge of English often leads to frustration and poor grades. With parents often working long hours, children sometimes turn to gangs to find protection and acceptance.

In their book *East to America: Korean American Life Stories*, authors Elaine H. Kim and Eui-Young Yu interviewed two young men who joined gangs. One of the men, Sean Suh, explains why he joined a gang. "They didn't know me; I was like the new kid in school. They used to get guys who knew everyone to pick on me to help their self-esteem at my expense. But when I got into the gang, I did it right back to them."

For Suh, joining a gang was a way to escape persecution. Getting out of the gang was much more difficult. But Suh offers some advice. "To get out of a gang, you've got to grow up and learn life. Most gangsters are smart enough to become doctors, but they never get the chance to grow up because they're either dead or in jail. They don't even know the possibilities for them."

while knowing underneath that I'd have to reconcile myself, to try to figure out where I would fit in a society that never sanctioned that identity as a public possibility. Part of growing up in America meant denying my cultural and ethnic identity, and part of that meant negating my parents. I still loved them, but I knew they could not help me outside the home.[54]

A second ideological shift that may put *i-se* children at odds with their parents is Korean unification. For children that have never visited the homeland and have few ties to Korea, events on the other side of the globe hold little interest. Issues affecting the homeland do not carry the same gravity as those in America. As Americans, they are more interested in events occurring in America and do not always agree with the need to focus on Korean politics and events.

Other Koreans completely discard their Korean ethnicity, proclaiming themselves wholly American. One young immigrant expresses the strain between generations: "It was hard when I was growing up, having my mom be Korean and me being American, living in a culture that is not the same as hers."[55]

Uncertain Identities

While *il-chom-o-se* and *i-se* children possess some cultural ties to Korea through their families, adoptees sometimes struggle to define themselves as both Korean and American. Oftentimes adoptees are raised in Caucasian families, and they have little or no exposure to Korean culture, language, and ideology. Their experience has been wholly American. These children grow up belonging to neither the Caucasian society where they were raised nor the Korean society in which they were born.

Korean adoptees see themselves as American and usually identify themselves as white until they look in the mirror. Their exposure to Korean culture has been limited, and few have had an opportunity to learn about their homeland. Some of the adoptive parents of these children attempt to educate them about their native country. Other adoptive parents are uncomfortable with their children's background and are unwilling or unable to provide education. Adoption records contain little information or family history, and parents may be uncomfortable about answering questions about issues such as abandonment.

Ignorance of transracial adoption can create uncomfortable situations outside the home, too. These situations sometimes bring a number of stories and questions from strangers. Some Caucasians cannot look beyond dark hair and dark eyes to see the fully assimilated American. Korean adoptees are usually given European or American names and are sometimes questioned about their backgrounds. For instance, participants in a study conducted by Holt International indicated that they were often asked where they were born and who their real parents were. One woman indicated that strangers thought she was her father's mistress instead of his child. In another case, during a doctor's

Korean American adoptees play a traditional game at the Holt Heritage Camp in New Jersey. The camp helps adoptees to connect with their cultural heritage.

appointment, one Korean physician remarked how well the adoptee spoke English and asked how long he had been in this country. Furthermore, when one adoptee arrived at the post office to pick up a package, the employee scrutinized his identification. Commenting on the adoptee's American name, the postal worker indicated the Korean American was "lucky they allowed you to change your name to something easy."[56]

On the flip side, these adoptees do not fit into Korean society either. Many are shunned for having no knowledge of their cultural heritage or for not speaking Korean. When visiting the homeland, many

are treated as inferiors or told they are not really Koreans. In one survey, adoptees indicated they were treated rudely when they visited Korea and other Koreans realized they did not speak the language. One Korean American said in *Blue Dreams*, "They think of us as *koji* [beggars] when we visit Korea."[57]

Some adoptees even feel anger toward their adoption. Faced with discrimination, they feel robbed of their national identity. Preferring to call themselves abductees, they consider themselves torn from their homeland and denied the opportunity to grow up as Koreans. Some feel that as young adoptees, they were denied the right to make choices about their future. Theirs is a sense of loss for the culture they never experienced.

Not all adoptees have experienced struggles with identity or discrimination. In the Holt survey, most adoptees expressed gratitude to their birth mothers for the opportunity to grow up in America, and believed their lives would have been vastly different had they remained in Korea. Many proudly embrace both their American and Korean heritage.

A New Hierarchy

While some Korean Americans lament the loss of their native culture, others wish to break free of all the old traditions. One of the challenges facing Korean American families is the change in the social hierarchy. First generation parents expect to maintain the old Confucian hierarchy, while their children seek the same freedom displayed by their American counterparts. This can lead to conflicts

An Adoptee's Journey

Kwang Wook Sohn was discovered on the steps of a police station in Seoul three days after his birth in 1974. He lived with a foster family in Korea until an American family adopted him at age five months. Raised in a rural midwestern town, he was given a Scottish American name and grew up as the only Korean for miles. In an interview with the author, Sohn describes his experiences growing up Korean American:

"I always knew I was adopted. It was obvious, since both my parents were Caucasian. But I grew up with a positive idea of being an adoptee. There was absolutely no Korean population where I grew up. My parents did not raise me knowing what Asian culture is. I see myself as an American—I'm an American born in Korea."

Asked about his experiences with stereotypes and discrimination, Sohn says, "Some people expected me to speak Korean, expected me to have Asian customs. My wife's grandparents asked if I celebrated Christmas. When she explained I grew up in a Christian Caucasian household, they still asked, 'But what is he?' Just because I look Asian does not mean I hold onto Asian customs. I never felt hostility or have been deliberately excluded because of my race. As a child I was called names. It hurt and made me upset. Every child is made fun of for some reason; that was just the reason people made fun of me. I still run into people who are ignorant in terms of not understanding. Nothing is done out of spite or to harm. Just curiosity. You still have people who make assumptions about you based on how you look."

While Sohn's experience has been positive, other adoptees are not so fortunate. Some face discrimination and ignorance, even from their families. As first generation immigrants, adoptees' stories are an important piece in the Korean American mosaic.

between parents demanding tradition and offspring desiring freedom. The American children may talk back to their parents or rebel against family rules as they desire to express their own thoughts and opinions. While this teenage behavior may sound typical, such outbursts are almost unheard of in a culture stressing respect for elders.

Children may develop an informality that disturbs their elders. Brenda Paik Sunoo describes her son David's response to the hierarchy in *East to America:* "One thing he just can't accept is the whole *hyong* [elder brother] thing. He absolutely refuses to kowtow to an older Korean just because he's older. He says a *hyong* has to earn his respect; he's not going to just give it to him because of his age."[58]

In addition to general behavioral differences, the emphasis on education is another friction point between generations. First-generation parents who have struggled to support their families demand that their children maintain good grades in order to attend college. The parents hope education will bring an easier life for their children. Children may not recognize their parents' struggle and feel satisfied receiving Bs on their report cards instead of As. Other students may feel guilty that their parents work long hours to send them to college. These children may forgo college as a means to spare their parents additional expense and sacrifice.

Society and Marriage

The Korean wedding tradition has also changed with Korean Americans. In Korea, weddings are complex affairs dictated by a series of rituals. It represents not only the union of a man and woman, but the joining of their families as well. In a traditional arrangement, a matchmaker uses a complex formula to determine a couple's compatibility. Figured into this equation are factors such as date, place, and time of birth, and even the components of the bride's and groom's names.

Today, marriage rules are more relaxed. While many Korean Americans now select their own spouse, a number of marriages are still arranged by the parents or conducted only after receiving final approval by the parents. In *East to America*, Kun Soo Kang compared marriage in the United States to the experience he and his wife encountered in Korea: "Here in America, they let their daughters marry men who are sincere, but in Korea they have to check to see if you have a house, money, a good job, and a good education. I didn't have any of those things." When he tried to discuss marriage with his wife's parents, "they locked her in and wouldn't even let her come to the telephone. I told them we would not break up and that we should all meet to discuss it, but they said there was nothing to talk about."[59]

According to the 2000 census data, 65 percent of Korean men choose Korean brides, while almost the same percentage of Korean women marry Caucasians. The increased number of interracial marriages shows an increased acceptance of Korean Americans. These mixed marriages also further incorporate Korean Americans into mainstream society.

Korean American Cultural Life

SIGNIFICANT LIFE EVENTS

First Birthday

On their first birthday, Korean American children are dressed in traditional clothing and given presents that signify their parents' wishes for their future –white rice bean cake, for a good clean life; string, for long life; a pencil and notepad, for education; and money, for wealth.

Marriage

Consistent with Confucian values, which emphasize honoring one's parents, Korean American newlyweds bow to their parents. The parents then throw dates and chestnuts at the bride and groom as symbols of the couple's future fertility.

Sixtieth Birthday

As people in old Korea rarely lived to the age of sixty, this is a milestone birthday in the life of Korean Americans, and an occasion for their children to throw the honored parent a lavish party.

Anniversary of Parent's Death

On the night before the anniversary of a parent's death, the children make different dishes as an offering to their deceased parent. The anniversary is observed on the night before the parent's passing, because it marks the last night the parent was alive to enjoy the offering.

ANNUAL CELEBRATIONS

Sollal (New Year's Day)

On the day before the first day of the first lunar month of the year, Korean Americans clean their parents' house and light candles throughout the night. On New Year's Day, they honor the spirits of their dead ancestors and prepare a special dumpling soup called *mandu gook*.

Buddha's Birthday

Although many Korean Americans are Christian, Buddha's birthday is still celebrated in Korea and in the United States with hundreds of lanterns and ceremonies to honor the faith of Buddhism.

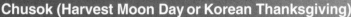

Chusok (Harvest Moon Day or Korean Thanksgiving)

On the fifteenth day of the eighth lunar month, Korean Americans prepare a special food called *songpyon,* which is made from rice powder, stuffed with bean filling, and then steamed and served with honey. On this day, Korean Americans give thanks for the kindness and good deeds of others.

Palioh (Independence Day)

On August 15, Korean Americans celebrate the end of World War II, when Korea achieved independence after thirty five years of Japanese colonial rule. Today, there are celebrations of Korea's unique cultural traditions in Koreatowns throughout the United States.

Cultural Rebirth

While the 1960s and 1970s were marked by a lull in Korean cultural education, interest in Korean culture has grown among Koreans and other ethnic groups in recent years. Across the country, exhibitions and museums highlight Korean American history. Korean American organizations have expanded to meet the need of the growing Korean population. Los Angeles alone has over 250 organizations that promote and support a variety of issues from education to politics.

In many cities, Korean churches and historical centers provide language lessons. They also sponsor programs exhibiting Korean dance, music, and art. Chicago hosts the annual Korean Street Festival in its Albany Park neighborhood. The Korean American Historical Society is dedicated to preserving the Korean American community's heritage. Other organizations like the Philip Jaisohn Memorial Foundation provide medical resources for the Korean American commu-

Interracial marriages between Korean women and Caucasian men are common. The practice helps many Korean Americans to assimilate into American society.

nity. Holt International organizes annual trips to Korea to help adoptees identify with their homeland and enable them to visit foster homes and orphanages.

Celebrating Korea's Heritage

Korean American families find ways to blend their past and present by observing traditional Korean holidays and celebrations. One such occasion is the *tol* celebration. In previous centuries, the prevalence of disease and absence of medical facilities resulted in a high mortality rate for Korean children. Many children died before their first birthday. When children reached their first year, the milestone was a time of thanks and celebration.

The *chut-tol*, or first birthday, is still celebrated by Korean American families. The *chut-tol* has four parts, each rich with symbolism. The child is dressed in a special costume called a *tol-bok*. Made from brightly colored silks, the *tol-bok* has a long sash, called a *tol-ddi*. The *tol-ddi* is wrapped around the child's waist twice to ensure long life. A small silken pouch, or *tol-jumuni*, is also worn to bring the child luck.

Prayer and thanks are a large part of the ceremony. Either the night before or early the morning of the birthday, a special prayer table is set. On the table are bowls of white rice, water, and mustard soup, along with a rice cake. The females of the family then offer prayers to the birth god, giving thanks for the healthy child.

The third phase is the preparation of the birthday table. Twelve different rice cakes (*ddeok*) are prepared and placed around the birthday child, along with an array of fruits and other foods. The highlight of the evening is the *toljabee*. During the *toljabee*, the child's future is divined. A selection of items is placed in front of the child, and his or her future occupation is determined depending on the objects he or she grabs. Rice indicates that the child will become wealthy, while a pen or brush indicates a future scholar. At the conclusion of the *toljabee*, the meal is shared with guests. Prayers are again given over the child, and gifts are presented. Gold rings are traditional gifts, to be used later for the child's education.

Another day in which children are celebrated is Children's Day. Observed on May 5, Children's Day is a time to honor one's children. Families usually spend the day at entertainment outlets such as parks, zoos, and amusement parks. The practice stems from the belief that children are necessary to ensure the survival of the family line. Korean Americans recognize the hope for the future in the new generation.

The balancing act between being Korean and being American, past and present, is an ongoing challenge for Korean Americans. In the past, mainstream America expected most immigrants to assimilate and give up their native culture. In the new century, however, more Americans are searching for their own cultural identifies, and interest in other cultures is increasing. Korean Americans can now educate and share their past with millions of Americans, bringing their unique perspective to America.

CHAPTER SEVEN

Korean American Contributions

K orean Americans are one of the fastest growing minority groups in the United States. According to the 2000 census, Koreans are the fifth largest group of immigrants entering the United States. As their population increases, more Korean Americans are moving into prominent professional positions and shining the spotlight on their community.

Since their first arrival in 1903, Korean Americans have actively worked to improve both their community and country. Many early immigrants found success despite discriminatory laws designed to limit their growth, rising to renown as doctors,

businessmen, and political figures. Today, changes in employment practices provide Korean Americans with opportunities to succeed in a variety of professions previously closed to them. From politics to entertainment, Korean American pioneers and standouts are finding acceptance in mainstream America. These men and women are role models not only to Korean Americans but also to young people in all walks of life.

Politics

For many years, Korean Americans had no representation in Congress. However,

Korean Americans are rapidly rising to political prominence. They are finding success as lawmakers, lawyers, and judges, careers denied them a half century ago. One such example is Judge Herbert Y.C. Choy. Choy was born on the Hawaiian island of Kauai in 1916. The son of plantation workers, he was the first Asian American to hold a seat in a federal court. After graduating from the University of Hawaii in 1938, Choy went on to Harvard Law School, where he graduated in 1941. Choy served in the army during World War II, achieving the rank of lieutenant colonel. After the war, Choy moved into private practice, becoming America's first Korean American lawyer. In 1971, President Richard Nixon named him to the Ninth Circuit Court of Appeals.

Another Korean American lawmaker is Senator John Lim. Lim was born in Yeoju, Korea, in 1935. His father was killed during the Korean War, leaving the family in a state of turmoil. As the man of the house, young John put his education on hold and went to work. He taught himself English by memorizing an English-Korean dictionary.

After returning to school, Lim earned a degree from Seoul Theological College in 1964. He immigrated to the United States in 1966 and attended school in Oregon. He and his wife ran a number of small businesses, and he later returned to school to study political science at Portland State University. Lim be-

came active in the Korean American community, serving as president of the Korean Society of Oregon and as national president of the Federation of Korean Associates, U.S.A.

His interest in public service led to politics. In 1990, Lim ran for governor of Oregon and received 11 percent of the popular vote. In 1992, Lim ran again for office, this time for the Oregon state senate. He was elected and served two terms

Republican senator John Lim was the first Korean American to win the nomination to the U.S. Senate.

in office. In 1998, Lim became the first Korean American to win the nomination to the United States Senate.

The Military

At the beginning of World War II, young Korean Americans flocked to U.S. military recruitment centers ready to fight for both the homeland and America. Although "Orientals" were barred from military service, Korean Americans still offered their lives for their country. Many viewed enlistment as doing their part to secure the homeland's freedom. Others expressed a desire to protect America. Throughout both World War II and the Korean War, Korean Americans distinguished themselves with their valor, whether on the battlefront or at home in intelligence operations. With American troops still stationed in Korea, Korean Americans continue to prove invaluable to the U.S. military.

One of the first Korean American war heroes, Young Oak Kim, was already a private first class in the army at the start of the war. He was accepted into officer candidate school, and in 1943 Kim joined the One Hundredth Infantry Battalion as a second lieutenant. The One Hundredth mostly consisted of Japanese soldiers. Understanding the long-standing animosity between the

Susan Ahn Cuddy was the first Asian American to join the navy. After her military career, she became involved with many Korean American civic organizations.

Japanese and Koreans, his colonel offered to arrange a transfer. Kim refused, believing that all the soldiers were Americans regardless of their cultural background.

In 1943, while the One Hundredth was in Italy, Kim was wounded by enemy fire. Despite his injuries, he continued throwing hand grenades across enemy lines until he was rescued. Kim was also instrumental in planning an attack on enemy forces at Anzio in 1944. After World War II, Kim served in Korea as a captain for the Thirty-first Infantry Regiment. His actions in Korea led to a promotion to major, and Kim became the first Asian American to command an American battalion.

The One Hundredth Infantry Battalion was the most decorated of World War II, and Kim was one of the most honored Asian Americans in American history. Kim received nineteen medals during his career. Among his many citations are two Silver Stars, the Distinguished Service Cross, two Legions of Merit, the Combat Infantryman Badge, two Bronze Stars, and three Purple Hearts.

In 1972, Kim retired from service with the rank of colonel. Kim continues to play an active role in the Korean American community. He is involved in the Go for Broke Educational Foundation, an organization founded by members of the 100th/442nd battallions to help educate teachers on their war experiences. He also supports the Korean Health Education Information and Research Center, a program that helps new Korean immigrants understand and obtain health care after their arrival in America. In 1999, Kim was also one of eight people asked to investigate re-ports that U.S. soldiers killed Korean civilians at No Gun Ri during the Korean War.

When asked about America's future, Kim states:

> We're a beacon for the rest of the world, but we have a long way to go. We have to continue to educate people not to be prejudiced and not to hate others. People today are less biased than people 25 years ago—that shows progress—and progress is hard to make. But I have great hopes for young people, and I am pleased with the young people I've met.[60]

Korean American women also joined the military. Susan Ahn Cuddy was the first Asian American to join the navy and became the first female gunnery officer in 1944. Public service was in her blood. She was born in Los Angeles in 1915, the third child of Korean patriot Ahn Chang-ho. She joined the navy in part to promote the Korean independence movement championed by her father. Although she was at first refused because of her race, Ahn Cuddy eventually earned an intelligence post. During World War II, she was a link trainer at Opalacca Naval Air Station in Florida, where she helped train pilots. She later joined the National Security Agency, retiring in 1959.

After her military career, Ahn Cuddy continued to be involved in a number of Korean American civic organizations, including the Korean American Heritage Foundation, the Patriot Ahn Chang-ho Memorial Foundation, and the Los Angeles 3.1 Woman's Association. In 2003, she received a Woman of the Year Award from the state of California. Her advice to other Korean Americans: "Embrace the country you're living in and never forget your Korean heritage. The best comes from combining the best of both cultures. It's magical."[61]

ABC News correspondent Juju Chang is a successful Korean American journalist.

The Media

Korean American public service extends beyond political and military careers and into high-profile occupations like the news media. Korean American broadcasters are visible every day on network television programs. The popularity of Korean American journalists is on the rise, not only in their own communities but throughout the rest of the United States as well. Two Korean American women in particular have attracted the nation's attention: Juju Chang and Lizabeth Cho.

Media correspondent Juju Chang was born in Seoul, South Korea, but raised in California. She studied political science and communications at Stanford University and was the recipient of the Edwin Cotrell Political Science Prize. In 1987, Chang was hired by ABC News. She reported numerous international stories, including the reburial of the Romanov family (Russia's last czar, his wife, and their children), and the U.S. embassy bombing in Kenya. During the early 1990s, she covered the Gulf War from Saudi Arabia. Chang may currently be seen on shows like *20/20*, *Good Morning America*, and *World News Tonight with Peter Jennings*.

Another Korean American journalist is ABC NewsOne Chicago's Lizabeth Cho. Born in Concord, Massachusetts, to a Korean father and an Austrian-Hungarian mother, Lizabeth attended Boston University where she studied broadcast journalism. She worked as a producer and editor for

New England Cable News before moving to Florida. In Miami, she reported various local and national stories for WPLG-TV. Her story on the Everglades was nominated for an Emmy Award in 1998. In 1999, Cho joined ABC NewsOne, where she has reported on a number of stories, including President Clinton's impeachment and George W. Bush's presidential campaign. In addition to NewsOne, Cho is also a coanchor for World News Now.

Sports

While some Korean Americans are winning fans through their intelligence and dedication to the community, others are drawing admirers with their athletic ability. Some sports personalities have followed in the footsteps of Sohn Kee-chung and Nam Sung-yong, winning Olympic gold. Others have risen to prominence in mainstream professional sports like hockey and golf.

One of the most famous Korean American athletes is the multifaceted Sammy Lee. Born in Fresno, California, in 1920, Lee is the son of Hawaiian plantation workers. In 1932, after seeing a display for the Olympic games in Los Angeles, Lee

Shown here diving at the 1952 Olympics, Sammy Lee was the first Asian American to win Olympic gold.

decided he wanted to one day become an Olympic champion. He first started diving at a recreation center in Los Angeles. In 1938, he met trainer Jim Ryan and began his quest for Olympic gold. Lee was the first man to win consecutive gold medals in the Olympic high diving event following his performances in the 1948 and 1952 games. Lee also earned another medal in 1952, a bronze in the three-meter springboard. He also made history by becoming the first Asian American to win gold. In

1953, he was honored with the James E. Sullivan Award for Outstanding American Athletics—the first non-Caucasian to ever receive the award. In 1968, Lee was inducted into the International Swimming Hall of Fame.

After his own career, Lee was the coach of the U.S. team from 1960 to 1964 and also trained silver medalist Greg Louganis for the 1976 Olympics. Later Lee was inducted into the U.S. Olympic Hall of Fame. Lee's dedication to youth in sports was recognized by his appointment in 1971 to the President's Council on Physical Fitness and Sports, a position he held until 1980. At age eighty-one, Lee was honored with a Lifetime Achievement Award from U.S. Divers, the governing body of American diving.

Hockey

The sport of ice hockey has been traditionally dominated by Caucasians. In 1991, Jim Paek made sports history by becoming the first Korean American to play in the National Hockey League (NHL). Born in Seoul in 1967, Paek had been a defenseman for the International Hockey League's (IHL) Muskegon Lumberjacks and the Canadian national team when he was called up by the Pittsburgh Penguins in 1991. That same year, the Penguins went on to win the Stanley Cup. Paek and the Penguins repeated their success in 1992, bringing the Stanley Cup to Pittsburgh for the second consecutive year. His breakthrough performance earned his Penguins jersey a spot in the Hockey Hall of Fame.

In 1993, Paek was traded to the Los Angeles Kings. Once again, Paek made it to the Stanley Cup finals, but the Kings were defeated by Montreal. In the following years Paek moved between several NHL and IHL teams and even played in England for the Nottingham Panthers. In 2003, Paek traded in his player status when he was named head coach of the Orlando Seals hockey team.

Golf

Korean American men are not the only ones finding renown in the sports world. Korean American women are achieving success on America's golf courses. Magazines like *Golf Digest* and numerous Web sites are exploring this phenomenon as Korean American women impress the golf world with their grace, poise, and power.

One of the most seasoned players on the LPGA (Ladies Professional Golf Association) circuit is Pearl Sinn-Bonanni. She was born in Seoul in 1967 but spent most of her life in America. She started playing golf when she was nine years old. Sinn-Bonanni attended Arizona State University, and in 1988 she won both the U.S. Women's Amateur Championship and the U.S. Women's Public Links titles. In 1990, she qualified for the LPGA in her first attempt. She was also a member of both the Curtis and World Cup teams. Her first LPGA win came in 1998 when she won the State Farm Classic. Sinn-Bonanni has also worked as a model for J. Lindeberg, has been a commentator for ESPN, and was on the LPGA Tour Executive Committee.

Michelle Wie

The world of golf has many stars, but none are rising as fast as Michelle Wie. Wie was born in Honolulu, Hawaii, on October 11, 1989. She started playing golf at the age of four, and by the age of eleven Wie had become the youngest girl to ever qualify for a U.S. Golf Association event.

At nearly six feet tall, Wie has earned a reputation for powerful drives, often launching the ball over three hundred yards. In 2004, Michelle became the youngest person and only the fourth woman to play in a Professional Golf Association (PGA) event when she played at the Sony Open. Although she missed the qualifying cut by one stroke, Wie still managed to outperform forty-seven men.

Nicknamed "The Big Wiesy," Wie is just beginning her career. Although she is still considered an amateur, Michelle's game has been receiving accolades from notable professionals. Golfer Fred Couples was quoted in *Golf World* as saying, "When you see her hit a golf ball . . .

Michelle Wie is one of the fastest rising stars in the sport of golf.

there's nothing that prepares you for it. It's just the scariest thing you've ever seen."

Californian Christina Kim is a newcomer to the LPGA and one of the youngest women currently on the tour. Kim was born in San Jose, California, in 1984. After winning the National High School Open Championship in 2000, Kim left high school early to pursue her professional career. She currently holds the record for the lowest score ever played in USGA (United States Golf Association) history when she shot a 62 at Indian Hills Country Club in 2001. In 2004, she shot another 62 during the State Farm Classic. Although Kim has yet to win a tournament, she had four top ten finishes by September 2004, earning more than three hundred thousand dollars. In fact, she was one of the top fifty-one money earners in 2003. Her outstanding performance has definitely made her an athlete to watch.

Literature

Korean Americans are finding success in academia as well as in athletics. With the traditional emphasis placed on scholarship, it is no wonder Korean American authors are finding critical acclaim. From novelists to autobiographers, Korean American writers are known for weaving tales of loss, hardship, and growth with grit and beauty. Books such as those by Gloria Hahn and Younghill Kang describe the difficulties of adjusting to life in America.

Author Richard E. Kim received rave reviews for his first book, *The Martyred*, a tale of wartime suffering. Born in Korea in 1932, Kim served in the Korean military until he came to the United States to go to school. He studied at Middlebury College in Vermont. After obtaining three master's degrees, he taught college courses, first at Long Beach State College and then at the University of Massachusetts. After *The Martyred*, Kim published two additional works, *Lost Names*, an account of the Japanese occupation, and *The Innocent*.

Like Kim, writer An Na has recently received acclaim for her first novel, *A Step from Heaven*. The story chronicles the life of a Korean family as they struggle to survive in America. Na's gritty novel shows the development of her heroine, Young Ju, from her arrival in America at age four until her departure for college. The family must cope with poverty, abuse, and alcoholism. Na's touching story has been nominated for dozens of awards, including the National Book Award and the Children's Book Award in Young Adult Fiction. It was the 2002 winner of the Michael Printz Award, which recognizes excellence in children's literature. The author was born in Korea but grew up in San Diego. She received her bachelor's degree from Amherst College and her master of fine arts degree from Vermont College.

Music

In addition to their achievements in literature, Korean Americans are gaining notoriety for their stellar performances in classical music. The talented Chung Trio has been winning audiences for over thirty years with their musical abilities. The trio consists of Myung-Whun on piano and his sisters Kyung-Wha (violin) and Myung-Wha (cello). All started playing between the ages of four and six, and each made their concert debuts before the age of ten. After the trio moved to America with their parents in 1961, they studied at the Juilliard School, the prestigious music, drama, and dance conservatory in New York City. Since completing their musical studies, the Chung Trio has released several albums and traveled the world.

In addition to their joint collaborations, each member of the trio has found success as a solo artist. Kyung-Wha won the prestigious Edgar M. Leventritt Competition at age nineteen and has since won Korea's Medal of Civic Merit, South Korea's highest honor. She has played with the London Symphony Orchestra, the New York Philharmonic, and the Seoul Philharmonic Orchestra. Cellist Myung-Wha has gained equal renown, playing venues as diverse as Florence, Italy; Hanoi, Vietnam; and Geneva, Switzerland. Their brother

Although they were trained as classical musicians, the Ahn Trio's hip approach to music and fashion has turned them into icons of American pop culture.

Myung-Whun has turned his focus to conducting, working with great orchestras around the world, including ones in Chicago, Illinois; Berlin, Germany; Boston, Massachusetts; and Vienna, Austria. He is the recipient of numerous music awards and has also served as a United Nations drug control ambassador and as Korea's honorary cultural ambassador.

Following in the Chung Trio's footsteps is another set of siblings, the Ahn sisters. Gorgeous and talented, the Ahn Trio is composed of twins Maria and Lucia on cello and piano and younger sister Angella

on violin. The sisters were born in Seoul, South Korea, and each started her musical career playing piano. The trio's first public appearance was on a Korean television program in 1979. The trio moved to the United States with their parents in 1981, and all attended Juilliard.

The Ahn Trio first gained notoriety after appearing in an issue of *Time* in 1987. Known for their hip wardrobe (they frequently wear leather pants and tank tops on stage) and fresh approach to music (the sisters have performed rock classics such as The Doors' "Riders on the Storm"), the award-winning trio has appeared on MTV as well as on PBS. Their unique fashion sense has earned them modeling contracts for clothing lines like the Gap and Anne Klein. They have also appeared in numerous magazines, such as *Vogue* and *Town and Country*, and were on the list of *People* magazine's fifty most beautiful people. The Ahn Trio's innovative approach to their craft has introduced classical music to a whole new world of listeners.

Margaret Cho is one of the most successful stand-up comics in the United States.

Film and Theater

In addition to their musical accomplishments, Korean Americans are finding visibility in theater and film. In the last decade, the entertainment industry incorporated more ethnic roles into productions to better reflect America's diverse population. While there are still a large number of Asian American gangsters in film and television, studios are working to provide more positive depictions of Korean Americans. With a wider variety of roles and the rise in popularity of all Asian productions, Korean American entertainers are growing in fame and popularity.

One of the most respected Korean American actors is Randall Duk Kim. Born in Hawaii, Kim is a highly acclaimed Shakespearean actor. His first foray onto the stage was at the age of eighteen when he performed the role of Malcolm in *Macbeth*. He later studied at the Guthrie Theatre in Minneapolis, where he performed the title role in *Hamlet*. Kim's other Shakespearean roles include Richard III, King Lear, King John, Titus Andronicus, Romeo, and Prospero.

In addition to his Shakespearean roles, he has also performed in Christopher Marlowe's *Tamberlaine the Great* and works by Anton Chekhov, Henrik Ibsen, and French playwright Molière. Kim's work in cinema includes roles in *The Replacement Killers*, *Anna and the King*, and as the Keymaker in *Matrix Reloaded.* He is the cofounder of the American Players Theater in Wisconsin and was the recipient of an Obie Award for Sustained Excellence of Performance in theater.

Another prominent Korean American actor is comedian Margaret Cho. Born Cho Mo-ran on December 5, 1968, Cho was raised by her parents in San Francisco. Her parents owned a bookstore, and her first attempt at stand-up was at age sixteen in a small theater called the Rose and Thistle, located above her parents' shop.

In the early days of her career, Cho won a comedy contest and opened for Jerry Seinfeld. She also appeared on *Arsenio Hall* and a Bob Hope special. Recognizing her talent, ABC gave Cho her own sitcom, *All American Girl.* The show illustrated the challenges encountered by a young woman balancing the expectations of her traditional Korean parents with her own mainstream American attitude. Although it lasted only one season, *All American Girl* was the first television program to feature an all-Asian cast.

After the end of her sitcom, Cho returned to stand-up. Since then, she has had three sold-out national tours and has had two feature films, *I'm the One That I Want* and *Notorious C.H.O.*, both of which have received critical acclaim. Offstage, Cho is active in promoting equal rights for Asian Americans and is also a crusader for gay and lesbian rights.

Another Korean American enjoying the spotlight is actor John Cho. Cho was born

Daniel Dae Kim has appeared on several popular television series, including Angel, Lost, *and* Buffy the Vampire Slayer.

in Seoul, South Korea, on June 16, 1972. Raised in Los Angeles, Cho graduated from the University of California at Berkeley with a degree in English literature. He started his acting career in 1996 with small roles on the television series *Boston Common.* He also appeared in *Charmed* and *Felicity.* In 2001, Cho played the part of Chau Presley in the series *Off-Centre.*

Cho later found work in movies, appearing in *Solaris*, *American Beauty*, and all three *American Pie* films. His most visible role was as Harold Lee in the 2004 release *Harold and Kumar go to White Castle.* Director Danny Leiner said of the film, "It turns a lot of stereotypes on their heads. It's really fun to watch them react to racist people who they come against, and just how people treat them, and how they're perceived by the culture and how they feel about it."[62]

Young audiences recognize actor Daniel Dae Kim for his role as Gavin Park on the television shows *Angel* and *Buffy the Vampire Slayer.* Born in Pusan, South Korea, Kim immigrated to Portland, Oregon, with his family when he was two. He received degrees in theater and political science and studied at the National Theater Institute in Connecticut. In 1996, he received a master's degree from the Tisch School of the Arts at New York University.

Kim has appeared in a number of movies and television productions, including guest spots on *ER*, *Enterprise*, *24*, *Charmed*, and the 2004 summer blockbuster *Spider-Man 2*, where he played Dr. Octopus's assistant, Raymond. Kim is also active in theater, appearing as Prospero in an all-Asian performance of *The Tempest.* His most recent role is in the ABC television series *Lost*, about a group of airline passengers stranded on an island after a crash.

The roles of Korean Americans have changed significantly in the last century. The high-profile careers of many Korean Americans prove they have gained acceptance within the mainstream American culture. Whether they find careers in business, politics, sports, or entertainment, Korean Americans are achieving success in America.

One Hundred Years of Korean Americans

On January 13, 2003, President George W. Bush commemorated the one-hundred-year anniversary of Korean immigration, stating:

> For the past century, Korean immigrants and their descendants have helped build America's prosperity, strengthened America's communities, and defended America's freedoms. . . . We acknowledge and commend Korean Americans for their distinguished achievements in all sectors of life and for their important role in building, defending and sustaining the United States of America.[63]

Conditions for Korean Americans have improved significantly in the past century. No longer forced to remain in difficult, low-wage jobs, Korean Americans are moving to the forefront of the American consciousness.

A Changing View

The perception of Korean Americans has changed significantly in the last century. As stereotypes are proven false and fade, Americans realize that Koreans are not the Yellow Peril threat of the early twentieth century, nor are they the crazed shopkeepers of the Los Angeles riots. Korean

Americans are gaining increased visibility and admiration through their strength and hard work. The continued growth of Korean Americans in professional fields is proof of their skill and determination. In a recent survey, 27 percent of Korean Americans were employed in highly skilled occupations, compared to 21 percent of Caucasian Americans.

But Korean Americans have yet to find equality. An estimated 43 percent of Korean Americans have college degrees, almost twice that of Caucasian Americans.

According to 2000 census data, Korean American families are among the highest wage earners of any ethnic American group. Despite these findings, their personal incomes are significantly lower than Caucasians. Korean Americans individually earn almost seven thousand dollars less than their white counterparts. In fact, Koreans have almost the lowest personal income of any Asian group, although their education level is among the highest.

Stereotypes and cultural boundaries continue to prevent mobility. Approxi-

As opportunities in many diverse fields continue to open to Korean Americans, the future looks very bright for this young Korean American girl.

mately 32 percent of Korean Americans do not possess fluency in English. This may prevent educated Korean Americans from stepping into high-wage jobs. Their high rate of self-employment also contributes to long hours and lower wages, as entire families work with little or no pay in order to support the business.

The Future of Korean Americans

The future for America's Koreans is brightening. Entrance rates of Korean American students into universities is rapidly increasing. Korean Americans are one of the most visible groups on college campuses nationwide. The traditional emphasis on scholarship is poising Korean American children to be America's next leaders, and the Korean American community is reaching out to help students achieve their goals.

For example, for almost twenty years, the Korean American Students Conference (KASCON) has brought together Korean students and leaders in education, business, and politics. The conference provides opportunities for Korean students to network with experts in professional fields and provides seminars on skills and job placement. Events like KASCON provide young Korean Americans with the tools necessary to become the leaders of tomorrow. Former New Jersey governor Christine Todd Whitman said in 2000 at KASCON XIV, "America will only grow more tolerant when leaders from every race, creed, ethnicity, and gender are serving at every office level from the local to the White House. I want to see that day because that will be the day when America will realize its full potential . . . as leaders not only in the Korean community, but also in the American family."[64]

With their knowledge of English combined with their education, more young Korean Americans will overcome the hurdles placed before their parents. In the coming years, the number of successful Korean Americans will increase, allowing them to become not only leaders of the Korean community but of the collective American community as well. In addition to their increased prosperity, they will shatter the negative stereotypes attributed to their community and become a powerful force in sculpting America's future.

NOTES

Chapter One:
Battle for the Hermit Kingdom

1. Bruce Cumings, *Korea's Place in the Sun: A Modern History*. New York: W.W. Norton, 1997, p. 100.
2. Quoted in Bong-Youn Choy, *Koreans in America*. Chicago: Nelson-Hall, 1979, p. 46.
3. Quoted in Ronald Takaki, *Strangers from a Different Shore*. Boston: Little, Brown, 1989, p. 55.
4. Quoted in Cumings, *Korea's Place in the Sun*, p. 115.
5. Quoted in Cumings, *Korea's Place in the Sun*, p. 117.
6. Bong-Youn Choy, *Koreans in America*, p. 35.
7. Quoted in Takaki, *Strangers from a Different Shore*, p. 56.
8. Mary Paik Lee, *Quiet Odyssey: A Pioneer Korean Woman in America*. Seattle: University of Washington Press, 1990, p. 60.
9. Quoted in Takaki, *Strangers from a Different Shore*, p. 54.

Chapter Two: A New Beginning

10. Quoted in Wayne Patterson, *The Korean Frontier in America: Immigration to Hawaii, 1896–1910*. Honolulu: University of Hawaii Press, 1988, p. 45.
11. Quoted in Bong-Youn Choy, *Koreans in America*, p. 75.
12. Quoted in Patterson, *The Korean Frontier in America*, p. 49.
13. Quoted in Patterson, *The Korean Frontier in America*, p. 95.
14. Quoted in Sucheng Chan, *Asian Americans: An Interpretive History*. Boston: Twayne, 1991, pp. 109–10.
15. Quoted in Bong-Youn Choy, *Koreans in America*, p. 321.
16. Quoted in Bong-Youn Choy, *Koreans in America*, p. 295.
17. Quoted in Takaki, *Strangers from a Different Shore*, p. 135.
18. Quoted in Takaki, *Strangers from a Different Shore*, p. 158.
19. Quoted in Bong-Youn Choy, *Koreans in America*, p. 295.
20. Quoted in Takaki, *Strangers from a Different Shore*, p. 135.
21. Quoted in Takaki, *Strangers from a Different Shore*, p. 135.
22. Quoted in Chan, *Asian Americans*, p. 109.

Chapter Three:
The Mainland and Discrimination

23. Quoted in Bong-Youn Choy, *Koreans in America*, p. 127.
24. Quoted in Bong-Youn Choy, *Koreans in America*, p. 127.
25. Quoted in Takaki, *Strangers from a Different Shore*, p. 273.
26. Lee, *Quiet Odyssey*, p. 15.
27. Quoted in Takaki, *Strangers from a Different Shore*, p. 271.
28. Quoted in Takaki, *Strangers from a Different Shore*, p. 271.

29. Quoted in Bong-Youn Choy, *Koreans in America*, pp. 109–10.
30. Easurk Emsen Charr, *The Golden Mountain: The Autobiography of a Korean Immigrant, 1895–1960*. Urbana: University of Illinois Press, 1961, p. 138.
31. Lee, *Quiet Odyssey*, pp. 16–17.
32. Lee, *Quiet Odyssey*, pp. 16–17.
33. Quoted in Nazli Kibria, *Becoming Asian American*. Baltimore: Johns Hopkins University Press, 2002, p. 176.
34. Charr, *Golden Mountain*, p. 192.

Chapter Four: Building Communities

35. Quoted in H. Brett Melendy, *Asians in America*. Boston: Twayne, 1977, p. 163.
36. Quoted in Takaki, *Strangers from a Different Shore*, p. 164.
37. Quoted in Takaki, *Strangers from a Different Shore*, p. 173.

Chapter Five: The Second Wave

38. Elaine H. Kim and Eui-Young Yu, *East to America: Korean American Life Stories*. New York: New Press, 1996, p. 360.
39. Quoted in Kim and Yu, *East to America*, pp. 74–75.
40. Quoted in Nancy Abelmann and John Lie, *Blue Dreams: Korean Americans and the Los Angeles Riots*. Cambridge, MA: Harvard University Press, 1995, p. 126.
41. Quoted in Kibria, *Becoming Asian American*, p. 62.
42. Quoted in Kim and Yu, *East to America*, p. 40.
43. Quoted in Kim and Yu, *East to America*, pp. 38–39.
44. Quoted in Abelmann and Lie, *Blue Dreams*, p. 37.
45. Quoted in Kim and Yu, *East to America*, p.16.
46. Ronald Takaki, *A Different Mirror: A History of Multicultural America*. Boston: Little, Brown, 1993, p. 4.
47. Quoted in Abelmann and Lie, *Blue Dreams*, p. 40.
48. Quoted in Kim and Yu, *East to America*, p. 39.
49. Quoted in Abelmann and Lie, *Blue Dreams*, p. 38.

Chapter Six: Becoming Korean American

50. Quoted in Elaine H. Kim, Lilia Villanueva, and Asian Women United of California, *Making More Waves: New Writing by Asian American Women*. Boston: Beacon, 1997, p. 69.
51. Quoted in Abelmann and Lie, *Blue Dreams*, p. 78.
52. Quoted in Kibria, *Becoming Asian American*, p. 36.
53. Quoted in Kim and Yu, *East to America*, p. 89.
54. Quoted in Cumings, *Korea's Place in the Sun*, p. 450.
55. Quoted in Kim and Yu, *East to America*, p. 145.
56. Kwang Wook Sohn, interview with author, El Paso, TX, August 12, 2004.
57. Quoted in Abelmann and Lie, *Blue Dreams*, p. 79.
58. Quoted in Kim and Yu, *East to America*, p. 150.
59. Quoted in Kim and Yu, *East to America*, p. 327.

Chapter Seven:
Korean American Contributions

60. Quoted in Joyce Caoile, "Colonel Young Oak Kim—the Most Decorated Soldier of the 100th/442nd Continues to Inspire," Asians in America Project, August 2003. www.asiansin america.org.

61. Quoted in Eurie Chang, "Susan Ahn Cuddy—a Korean American Pioneer Who Broke Racial and Gender Barriers During WW II," Asians in America Project, May 2004. www.asiansin america.org.

62. Quoted in Chris Jordan, "'Harold' Takes on Asian stereotypes," *El Paso (Texas) Times*, August 3, 2004.

Epilogue: One Hundred Years of Korean Americans

63. Quoted in Richard Tomkins, "Bush Honors Korean Immigration," United Press International, January 13, 2003. www.upi.com/view.cfm?Story ID=20030113-041452-9154r.

64. Quoted in the KASCON XVII prospectus, Cornell University, March 13–16, 2003. www.kascon.com/media.

FOR FURTHER READING

John Cha, *Willow Shade Tree: The Susan Ahn Cuddy Story.* Malibu, CA: Island Mountain Trading, 2003. This biography details Cuddy's struggle against racism and war. The daughter of patriot Ahn Chang-ho, Cuddy seeks to define herself as her own person as well as her father's daughter.

Jenny Ryun Foster, *Century of the Tiger: One Hundred Years of Korean Culture in America, 1903–2003.* Honolulu: University of Hawaii Press, 2003. This book contains several Korean accounts, from life in Korea to living in Hawaii during World War II. The narrative is enhanced by numerous glossy pictures of Korean artwork, historical documents, and photographs.

Patrick D. Joyce, *No Fire Next Time: Black-Korean Conflicts and the Future of America's Cities.* Ithaca, NY: Cornell University Press, 2003. Joyce discusses the roots of black–Korean conflicts, comparing the nonviolent protests of New York City with the devastation in Los Angeles.

An Na, *A Step from Heaven.* Asheville, NC: Front Street, 2001. In this fictional account, Young Ju and her family struggle to survive after coming to America. In addition to the challenge of acculturation, Young Ju's family struggles against alcoholism and abuse. This book follows Young Ju from age four to her departure for college.

Linda Sue Park, *When My Name Was Keoko.* New York: Clarion, 2002. This semiautobiographical novel is based on the author's experiences growing up in Japanese-occupied Korea. Sun-hee and her brother Tae-yul struggle to maintain their Korean identity as their customs, language, and names are stolen. This is a touching story of one family's sacrifice during the years of occupation.

WORKS CONSULTED

Books

Nancy Abelmann and John Lie, *Blue Dreams: Korean Americans and the Los Angeles Riots*. Cambridge, MA: Harvard University Press, 1995. Filled with many personal accounts, this book discusses the events of the Los Angeles riots. Interviews with Korean Americans give insights into their hopes and dreams and the conflicts leading to the riots.

Lan Cao and Himilce Novas, *Everything You Need to Know About Asian-American History*. New York: Plume, 1996. Presented as a series of questions and answers, this book provides a brief overview of Asian American history. Sidebars provide Asian American statistics and lists of famous Asian Americans.

Sucheng Chan, *Asian Americans: An Interpretive History*. Boston: Twayne, 1991. Chan's book provides a comprehensive overview of Asian American immigration. She compares the different motivations and experiences of each Asian group in a compelling and respectful fashion.

Easurk Emsen Charr, *The Golden Mountain: The Autobiography of a Korean Immigrant, 1895–1960*. Urbana: University of Illinois Press, 1961. One of the first Korean immigrants to publish an autobiography, Charr discusses his experiences in Korea and America. His humble and moving account details the determination of one person to build a good life in America.

Bong-Youn Choy, *Koreans in America*. Chicago: Nelson-Hall, 1979. One of the earliest books on Korean American history, Choy's provides a very thorough and scholarly account. He uses quotes throughout, and the oral histories included at the end are excellent.

Bruce Cumings, *Korea's Place in the Sun: A Modern History*. New York: W.W. Norton, 1997. Cumings provides the complex history of Korea in an educational but familiar style. His clever insights make for an enjoyable read.

Nazli Kibria, *Becoming Asian American*. Baltimore: Johns Hopkins University Press, 2002. Focusing on Korean and Chinese immigrants, Kibria enlivens survey data with personal accounts of Korean and Chinese Americans.

Elaine H. Kim, Lilia Villanueva, and Asian Women United of California, *Making More Waves: New Writing by Asian American Women*. Boston: Beacon, 1997. This anthology contains stories, poems, articles, and interviews created by Asian American women. It offers a perspective of the unique issues facing Asian women in America.

Elaine H. Kim and Eui-Young Yu, *East to America: Korean American Life Stories*. New York: New Press, 1996. A compilation of various Korean American accounts from monk to gang member, Kim and Yu provide an emotional and satisfying volume.

Elizabeth Kim, *Ten Thousand Sorrows*. New York: Doubleday, 2000. A heart-wrenching and controversial autobiography, the book starts with Kim's childhood in Korea. Despite ridicule from neighbors, she and her mother lead a contented life. After her mother's murder, Kim endures abuse and neglect from her adopted family and husband. A truly remarkable story of growth and survival.

Hyung-Chan Kim and Wayne Patterson, *The Koreans in America, 1882–1974: A Chronology and Fact Book*. New York: Oceana, 1974. A concise account of Korean American history. This timeline includes birthdays of prominent Korean Americans and notable dates in Korean American history.

Mary Paik Lee, *Quiet Odyssey: A Pioneer Korean Woman in America*. Seattle: University of Washington Press, 1990. Lee's family fled Korea as political refugees. One of the earliest Korean families to arrive in America, they struggled to find work and acceptance. An inspiring story of one family's struggle against poverty and hatred.

Donald Stone MacDonald, *The Koreans: Contemporary Politics and Society*. Boulder, CO: Westview, 1990. A history of Korea covering the last two thousand years, this book includes customs, religion, politics, and history from the earliest kingdom to the present.

H. Brett Melendy, *Asians in America*. Boston: Twayne, 1977. Melendy's book covers only Korean, Filipino, and East Indian immigrants. He provides a brief overview of homeland conditions, struggles for acceptance, and the building of Asian American communities.

Wayne Patterson, *The Korean Frontier in America: Immigration to Hawaii, 1896–1910*. Honolulu: University of Hawaii Press, 1988. This is a study of the conditions leading to Korean immigration, with a focus on Korean and American politics. Includes accounts of Korean immigrants.

Ronald Takaki, *A Different Mirror: A History of Multicultural America*. Boston: Little, Brown, 1993. Takaki's book provides information on a variety of immigrant groups. Readers can gain insight into the challenges encountered by immigrants at different times.

————, *Strangers from a Different Shore*. Boston: Little, Brown, 1989. A wonderful overview of Asian American immigration, this book is filled with compelling quotes from settlers. Broken into sections by culture, it can be read in parts but is most informative when read chronologically.

Interview

Kwang Wook Sohn, interview with author, El Paso, TX, August 12, 2004.

Periodical

Chris Jordan, "'Harold' Takes on Asian Stereotypes," *El Paso (Texas) Times*, August 3, 2004.

Internet Sources

ABCNews.com, "Juju Chang." http://abcnews.com/sections/2020/2020/chang_juju_bio.html.

The Ahn Trio, "Once UpAhn a Time." www.ahntrio.com.

AsianInfo.org, "Challenges of Modernization: Response to Capitalist Encroachment." www.asianinfo.org/asianinfo/korea/history/challenges_of_moderni zation.html.

"Asian-Pacific Americans in the U.S. Army," U.S. Army Center of Military History. www.army.mil/cmh-pg/topics/apam/ap.html.

Asia Source, "The Impact of the Los Angeles Riots on the Korean-American Community," May 3, 2002. www.asiasource.org/news/at_mp_02.cfm?newsid=79441.

———, "Syngman Rhee (Yu Sung-man; 1875–1965)," 2003. www.asiasource.org/society/syngmanrhee.cfm.

Judith A. Berling, "Confucianism," AskAsia, 1996. www.askasia.org/frclasrm/readings/r000004.htm.

Joyce Caoile, "Colonel Young Oak Kim—the Most Decorated Soldier of the 100th/442nd Continues to Inspire," Asians in America Project, August 2003. www.asiansinamerica.org/museum/0803_museum.html.

Center for Korean American Studies, "Census Tables: Korean American Population in the U.S.," October 10, 2003. www.calstatela.edu/centers/ckaks/census_tables.html/museum/0504_museum.html.

Eurie Chang, "Susan Ann Cuddy—a Korean American Pioneer Who Broke Racial and Gender Barriers During WW II," Asians in America Project, May 2004. www.asiansinamerica.org/museum/0504_museum.html.

Kuei Chiu, "Asian Language Newspapers in the United States: History Revisited," University of California, Riverside, August 28, 1996. www.white-clouds.com/cala/publications/e-journal/ej9chiu.html.

Margaret Costa, "An Olympian's Oral History," Amateur Athletic Foundation of Los Angeles, December 1999. www.aafla.org.

Philip Ahn Cuddy, "Philip Ahn: Born in America," PhilipAhn.com, 1996. www.philipahn.com.

Daniel Dae Kim Web site, "Biography," www.danieldaekim.org/bio.html.

Eurasian Nation, "Lizabeth Cho." www.eurasiannation.com/generic120.html.

Global Korean Network of Los Angeles, "Dosan Changho Ahn." www.gknla.net/main/projects/history/dosan_intro.html.

Holt International Children's Services, "The Historical Context of International Adoption of Korean Children," September 1999. www.holtintl.org/pdfs/Survey2.pdf.

Bong H. Hyun, "The Life of Philip Jaisohn, M.D. (1864–1951)," Philip Jaisohn Memorial Foundation. www.jaisohn.org.

KASCON XVII Prospectus, Cornell University, March 13–16, 2003. www.kascon.com/media.

Brent Kelley, "Michelle Wie Biography," About.com. http://golf.about.com/cs/womensgolf/a/michellewie.html.

Randall Duk Kim Web site, "Randall Duk Kim," October 13, 2003. www.randalldukkim.com.

Kim Yoon-sik, "Centennial of Korean Immigration to America," *Korea Times*, January 5, 2003. http://times.hankooki.com/lpage/opinion/200301/kt2003010517501911390.html.

Korean American Political Action Committee, "Chronology of Korean American History (1864 to 2001)." www.kapac.org/history.html.

Korean Centennial 1903–2003, "War Hero Honored," November 6, 2001. www.koreancentennial.org/warhero.html.

Korean History Project, "The Oppert Affair." www.koreanhistoryproject.org/Ket/Idx/KETIndex2104.html.

Richard E. Lapchick, "Asian Sports Star and Athletes," Asian-Nation, 2003. www.asian-nation.org/sports.shtml 2003.

C.N. Le, "Interracial Dating and Marriage," Asian-Nation, August 12, 2004. www.asian-nation.org/interracial.shtml.

Yoon M. Lee, "Emergence of Organizations and Churches: Christians Set the Philosophical Foundation of Community." http://gort.ucsd.edu/jhan/ER/ka.html.

Mike Lewis, "Sohn Kee-chung: Korean Athlete Whose Olympic Protest Made Him a National Hero," *Guardian*, November 30, 2002. www.guardian.co.uk/print/0.3858.4557980-103684.00.html.

Life in Korea, "Child's First Birthday (Tol)." www.lifeinkorea.com/culture/tol/tol.cfm.

Heather MacDonald, "Why Koreans Succeed," *City Journal*, Spring 1995. www.city-journal.org/html/5_2_a2.html.

Margaret Cho official Web site, "Updated Biography," March 26, 2004. www.margaretcho.com.

Angela E. Oh, "Five Years Later, Korean Americans Still Feel Riot's Heat," *UCLA Today,* May 9, 1997. www.today.ucla.edu/1997/970509 FiveYears.html.

Oregon State Senate, "John Lim." www.leg.state.or.us/lim.

Sara Schonhardt, "A Penchant for Perfection," *Asia Times Online*, October 22, 2003. www.atimes.com/atimes/Korea/EJ22 Dg03.html.

Richard Tomkins, "Bush Honors Korean Immigration," United Press International, January 13, 2003. www.upi.com/view.cfm?StoryID=20030113-041452-9154r.

University of Southern California, "Koreatown Map Series." www.usc.edu/dept/CCR/ktown.html.

U.S. Census, "Asian and Pacific Islander Population," 2002 March CPS Report. www.census.gov/population/www/socdemo/race/api.html.

The WB.com, "John Cho: Cast Bio." www.thewb.com/Faces/CastBio/0,7930,251,00.html.

Index

adoption, of children
 after war, 61–63
 identity and, 76–78
Ahn Chang-ho, 42, 87
Ahn Cuddy, Susan, 86, 87–88
Ahn Jong-Su, 52
Ahn Trio, 93–94
Allen, Horace, 22–23, 25
alphabet, 48, 49
Amerasian Immigration Act of
 1982, 63
anniversary, of immigration,
 celebration of, 97
Asian discrimination
 anti-Chinese sentiment and,
  21–22
 history of, 6
 immigration to mainland
  and, 33
 Yellow Peril and, 34–37, 41,
  43
assimilation, 71, 72
athletes, 19, 89–90
authors, 92

birthdays, first, celebration of,
 83
Briseno, Theodore, 67
broadcasters, 88–89
Bush, George W., 97
business
 opportunity in, 64–66, 98–99
 riots and, 67–69
 in South Central Los
  Angeles, 66–67
 see also sugar plantations

California

churches in, 46
discrimination in, 36–37
fear of Asian workers in, 34
immigration to, 34
interracial marriage in, 40
Koreatowns in, 71
Reedley, 71
South Central Los Angeles,
 66–69
Webb-Heney Land Law in,
 38–39
celebrations, 81, 83, 97
Chang, Juju, 88
Charr, Easurk Emsen, 37, 38,
 43
Chemulpo Treaty, 21
children
 adopted, 61–63, 76–78
 conflict between parents and,
  75–76, 78–79
 gangs and, 75
Children's Day, 83
China, 10, 11, 16
Chin 'mok-hoe, 42
Cho, John, 95–96
Cho, Lizabeth, 88–89
Cho, Margaret, 94, 95
Choe, Sara, 30
Ch'oe Che-u, 15, 16
Choi, Anna, 27
ch'ommin, 10
Choson, 8–9
Choy, Herbert Y. C., 85
Christianity
 churches and, 46–47
 in Korea, 11–12, 18–19, 24
 missionaries and, 25
 war brides and, 61

chungin, 9–10
Chung Trio, 92–93
churches, 46–47, 82
chu-tol, 83
citizenship
 denial of, 41, 43
 naturalization laws and,
  59–60
citrus groves, 34, 38, 39
classes, social, 9–10
 see also social structure
clothing, 36
 color of, 10
community
 beginnings of, 6–7
 church and, 46–47
 education and, 47–50
 family ties and, 52
 in Koreatowns, 7, 71–72
 lending system of, 50–51
 newspapers and, 51–52
 plantation society and, 44–46
 politics and, 52, 54
Confucianism
 ancestor worship and, 23
 Chinese emperor and, 11
 political relationships and,
  10
 social relationships and, 9
cultural life, 80, 82–83
cultural misunderstanding, 35

Deshler, David, 23, 24–25
division, of country, 58
Dong Hwan Ku, 65–66, 69
Donner, Francesca, 40, 41
Do-yun Yoon, 36–37
Duckworth, Yong, 51

East-West Development
    Company, 23
education
    churches and, 47
    conflict between children
        and parents over, 79
    employment level and,
        64–66
    in Hawaii, 47–49
    higher, 99
    on mainland, 49–50
employment
    in citrus groves, 34, 38, 39
    personal income and, 98–99
    small businesses and, 64–66
    see also farming; military
        service
entertainers, 94–96
Eui-Young Yu, 58–59

family ties, 52
farming, 14–15, 17–18, 19
Ferón, Stanislas, 13
first generation, 72–73
France, 12
future, as improving, 99

gangs, 75
gender separation, 25–26
General Sherman (ship), 13
generation
    first, 72–73
    one-and-a-half, 73–74
    second, 74–76
Go for Broke Educational
    Foundation, 87
golfers, 90–91
government, provisional, 54–55
grave robbing, 13
grocery stores, 64–66

hangul, 48, 49
Harlins, Latasha, 68

hats, 10
Hawaii
    churches in, 46
    immigration to, 24, 25–26,
        30
    United States and, 21
    see also sugar plantations
Hawaiian Sugar Planters'
    Association (HSPA), 22, 24,
    25
Hermit Kingdom nickname,
    8–9
Holt, Henry and Bertha, 62–63
Holt Heritage Camp, 77
Holt International, 83
Honokaa Plantation, 32
housing, 28–29, 30, 36

ice hockey players, 90
identity
    adoptees and, 76–78
    stereotypes and, 69, 97–98
    see also generation
il-chom-o-se, 73
il-se, 72–73
Immigration Act of 1965, 60
income, personal, 98
independence of homeland,
    movement for, 52–55
internment camps, 55
invasions of Korea, 11
i-se, 74–76
isolationism, 11

Japan
    annexation of Korea by,
        16–17
    attack on Pearl Harbor by, 55
    defeat of, in World War II, 57
    proximity to, 8
    rebellion against occupation
        of Korea by, 19–20
    reforms by, 17–19

sugar plantations and, 29–30
    trade with, 14
    workers from, in Hawaii, 22
Japanese and Korean Exclusion
    League, 37, 38
Jones, George Heber, 25
journalists, 88–89

Kang, Dredge, 74
Kibria, Nazli, 65
Kim, Christina, 91
Kim, Daniel Dae, 95, 96
Kim, Elaine, 75–76
Kim, Elizabeth, 64
Kim, Randall Duk, 94–95
Kim, Richard E., 92
Kim, Young Oak, 86–87
Kim Il-sung, 58
King, Rodney, 67, 69
KNA. *See* Korean National
    Association
Kojong (king)
    immigration to Hawaii and,
        23, 29
    taewon-gun and, 11
    Tonghak rebellion and, 16
    trade and, 12, 14
Konglip Sinbo (newsletter), 51
Koon, Stacey, 67
Korean-American Education
    Center, 50
Korean American Historical
    Society, 82
Korean American Students
    Conference, 99
Korean Compound School, 48
Korean Episcopal Church, 46
Korean Evangelical Society, 46
Korean Health Education
    Information and Research
    Center, 87
Korean Methodist Church, 46,
    48

Korean National Association
  (KNA), 45, 46, 52, 54
Korean National Herald
  (newspaper), 52
Korean War, 7, 57–59
Korean Youth Military
  Academy, 53
Koreatowns, 7, 71–72
Kun Soo Kang, 79
kye, 50–51

language
  education and, 50
  employment opportunity
    and, 65, 98–99
  first generation and, 72
  Japanese rule and, 18
  Koreatowns and, 71
  one-and-a-half generation
    and, 73
  second generation and,
    74–75
  xenophobia and, 36
Lee, David, 47
Lee, K.W., 67
Lee, Sammy, 89–90
Lee Nai-soo, 30
lending system, 50–51
Lim, John, 85–86
luna, 27

mainland, immigration to, 34
March First movement, 17,
  19–20
marriage
  interracial, 40, 79, 82
  to picture brides, 30–31, 41
  to war brides, 60–61, 62
  wedding tradition, 79
McCarran-Walter Immigration
  and Naturalization Act, 59
military academies, 53
military service, 55, 56, 86–88

Min (queen), 12, 22
missionaries, 25
model minority idea, 66
mothers, unwed, 62, 64
Mugunghwa School, 50
musicians, 92–94
Mutual Assistance Society, 42,
  46, 51
Myung-ja Sur, 20

Na, An, 92
names, 18
Nam Sung-yong, 19, 89
naturalization laws, 43, 59–60
New People's Society, 52
newspapers, 51–52
New York City, 71

Olympic athletes, 19
one-and-a-half generation,
  73–74
One Hundredth Infantry
  Battalion, 86–87
Oppert, Ernst, 13
orchards, 34, 35, 38
Oriental Exclusion Act, 40–41

Paek, Jim, 90
Paik Lee, Mary
  on housing conditions, 30,
    36
  on taunting, 37
  on treatment of Christians,
    18–19
Paik Sunoo, Brenda, 79
Park, Lisa, 73
Park Yong-man, 53, 54–55
Philip Jaisohn Memorial
  Foundation, 82–83
physicians, 65
picture bride system, 30–31, 41
plantations. See sugar
  plantations

political relationships, 10
politics, 52, 54, 84–86
population
  current, 7
  in Koreatowns, 71
  in 1985, 60
  by state, 72
  in 2000, 84
Powell, Laurence, 67
Price, Kyong-ae, 60, 62
professionals, as immigrants,
  63–64

quota system, 59, 60

racial discrimination
  banks and, 50
  in citizenship, 43
  Oriental Exclusion Act and,
    41
  Yellow Peril and, 34–37
  see also Asian discrimination
Reeley, California, 71
riots, in South Central Los
  Angeles, 67–69

sangmin, 10
second generation, 74–76
second wave, of immigration,
  59–60
See Hong-Ki, 27
Sejong the Great (king), 49
self-employment, 64–66
servitude, indentured, 23–24
Shinhan Minbo (newspaper),
  51–52
Sinn-Bonanni, Pearl, 90
social structure
  in America, 78–79
  half-American children and,
    62, 64
  in Korea, 9–10
  on sugar plantations, 26–27

Sohn, Kwang Wook, 78
Sohn Kee-chung, 19, 89
Soon Ja Du, 68–69
South Central Los Angeles, 66–69
Soviet Union, 57–58
sports figures, 89–90
stereotypes, 69, 97–98
Steward, Mary, 38, 39
sugar plantations
    camp conditions on, 28–29, 30
    education and, 49
    labor for, 21–23
    life on, 27
    social hierarchy on, 26–27
    society and, 44–46
    women on, 32
    work on, 27–28
Suh, Sean, 75
Sunjong (prince), 16–17
Syngman Rhee
    Korean Christian Institute and, 49
    life of, 48
    marriage of, 40, 41
    as minister, 47
    provisional government and, 54

taewon-gun (grand prince), 11, 13, 14
Tai Yoo Kim, 32
taxation, 14–15
Tiger Brigade, 56
tol celebration, 83
Tonghak rebellion, 15–16
tong-hoe, 45–46
topknot, 17
trade, with United States, 12–14
Treaty of Amity and Commerce, 14
Treaty of Kanghwa, 14

United Korean Committee, 56
United Korean Society, 46
United States
    Hawaii and, 21–22
    immigration to, 20
    trade and, 12–14

violence, against immigrants, 37–38, 67–69

war brides, 60–61, 62
Webb-Heney Land Law, 38–39
wedding tradition, 79

Western encroachment, 11–12
Whang Sa Sun, 35
Whitman, Christine Todd, 99
Wie, Michelle, 91
Wind, Timothy, 67
women
    golf and, 90–91
    as picture brides, 30–31, 41
    on sugar plantations, 32
    as unwed mothers, 62, 64
    as war brides, 60–61, 62
    in World War II, 20
World War II
    defeat of Japan and, 57
    Korean Americans during, 55–56
    One Hundredth Infantry Battalion in, 86–87
    women in, 20

yangban, 9, 10, 11, 17
Yang Choo-en, 28, 29
Yellow Peril, 34–37, 40–41
Yi Ha-ung, 11
Yoong Soon, 61
Yun Pyong-Ku, 52

PICTURE CREDITS

Cover: © Catherine Karnow/ CORBIS
AFP/Getty Images, 65
AP Wide World Photos, 77, 85, 86
AP/THE YORK DISPATCH, 94
© Bettman/ CORBIS, 17, 41, 61, 89
© Myrleen Ferguson Cate/ Photo Edit, 63
Courtesy of Roberta Chang/Willie Lee Album, 31
© CORBIS, 10, 15, 24, 28, 36
© Corel, 59, 81 (Buddha's Birthday and Palioh images)
Courtesy of Philip Cuddy, 12, 16, 18, 35, 42, 45, 53, 81 (Sollal and Chusok images)
Courtesy of Lisa Eastlack, 74, 80, 82
Courtesy of Arthur Elgort, 93
© Robert Galbraith/Reuters/ CORBIS, 91
© John Gaps III/ AP Wide World, 68
© Getty Images, 88
© Hulton-Deutsch Collection/ CORBIS, 54
© Steve Kagan/Time Life Pictures/Getty Images, 51
Courtesy of Dr. Anna Charr Kim, 38
© Lucidio Studio Inc./ CORBIS, 98
© Michael Maslan Historic Photographs/ CORBIS, 22
Courtesy of Presbyterian Historical Society, Presbyterian Church (U.S.A) (Philadelphia, PA), 23
© Reuters/ CORBIS, 20
© Ramin Talaie/ CORBIS, 7
© Time Life Pictures/ Getty Images, 67
© Frank Trapper/ CORBIS, 95
© Nik Wheeler/ CORBIS, 71
Steve Zmina, 49, 72, 80-81

ABOUT THE AUTHOR

Jennifer C. Martin was a business writer for three years before embarking on her freelance career. She and her husband, Christopher, live in central Illinois with two cats and a rabbit.

WITHDRAWN

The Columbus Academy
Reinberger Middle School Library
4300 Cherry Bottom Road
Gahanna, Ohio 43230